ENGLISH
for the
SPANISH SPEAKER

Book 4

Ages 10 - Adult

Written by

Kathleen Fisher

Fisher Hill   Huntington Beach   California

Copyright 1999, 2009 by Kathleen Fisher
First Printing 1999
Second Printing 2002
Third Printing 2004
Fourth Printing 2005
Fifth Printing 2009, revised
Printed in the United States of America
All rights reserved.

Published by FISHER HILL
5267 Warner Avenue, #166
Huntington Beach, CA 92649-4079

Publisher's Cataloging in Publication

Fisher, Kathleen S., 1952-
    English for the Spanish speaker. Book 4 / by Kathleen Fisher
        p. cm.
        Includes bibliographical references and index.
        Audience: Ages 10-adult.
        ISBN 978-1-878253-52-1

    1.   English language--Textbooks for foreign speakers--Spanish.   2. English as a second language.

PE1129.S8F58 2009 v.4   482.2'461

English for the SPANISH SPEAKER
Book 4

by
Kathleen Fisher

CONTENTS * MATERIAS

CONTENTS * MATERIAS

Teacher's Guide

Each lesson includes the following pages. Below are activities and ideas for each page.

Vocabulary Page
- Teacher, student helper, or tutor pronounces the English words and the students repeat.
- The words from the vocabulary list can be used for a weekly spelling test.
- Students write sentences or a story using the vocabulary words.

Conversation Page
- Teacher, student helper, or tutor reads the conversation in English and the students repeat.
- Students read the conversation together each taking a different part.

Story Page
- Teacher, student helper, or tutor reads one sentence at a time and the students repeat.
- Students read the story quietly to themselves.
- Students act out the story putting in their own English dialog.

Fill in the Blank and other Activity Pages
- Students do these pages on their own or in small groups.
- Different students go up to the board to write the answers while the other students correct their work.
- Students check their work with the **Answer Key.**

Puzzle Fun
At the end of the book are puzzles. Each one uses the vocabulary words from two lessons. (The first puzzle uses vocabulary words from Lessons 1 and 2.) These activities provide extra practice for the students.

Related Activities
- In small groups, students make up and put on short skits about the lesson's theme using English dialog.
- Students draw, paint, or create pictures about the lesson's theme and then explain or discuss their pictures in English.
- Students talk about their own personal experience as it relates to the lesson's theme.
- Students write about their own personal experience as it relates to the lesson's theme and then read their stories to the group.

English for the Spanish Speaker
Book 4

Instructions

This book was written to teach English to the person who can read, write, and speak Spanish. Book 4 presents intermediate English to help a person live and work in the United States.

Book 4 follows the general pattern of Books 1, 2 and 3. It is progressively more difficult. There are eight lessons and Puzzle Fun. Four lessons deal with every day themes, i.e., A Place to Live, A Visit to the Bank, etc. The other four lesson topics are on U.S. history and government. The lessons are presented in English and then translated into Spanish. All the instructions are in Spanish. Puzzle Fun includes crossword puzzles, jumbles, and wordsearches. At the end of the book are two dictionaries: English-Spanish and Spanish-English; and an index.

Each lesson is divided into several parts. First, there is a vocabulary list. Basic English words as well as the vocabulary of the particular theme are included in the list. Then there is a conversation in order to use the vocabulary in a common situation. Next is a story related to the theme which reinforces the vocabulary and the conversation. The fourth page of each lesson is an exercise that requires choosing a word from the vocabulary list and then writing it in a sentence that is missing one word. The next three pages are a variety of activity pages. And at the end of each lesson are the answers to the exercises so that the student will be successful.

It is recommended that the student do one lesson per week but the pupil can go through the book more rapidly if he or she so desires. The speed at which the student learns English depends on the student himself or herself. It would be useful to read the conversation and story out loud. This will help the pupil gain smoothness. A complete Spanish-English; English-Spanish dictionary should be the pupil's constant companion. The student

Inglés para el Hispanohablante
Libro 4

Instrucciones

Este libro fue escrito para enseñarle inglés a una persona siempre y cuando la persona pueda leer, escribir, y hablar español. El libro 4 presenta inglés intermedio para ayudar a la persona a vivir y a trabajar en los Estados Unidos.

El libro 4 generalmente sigue el modelo del Libros 1, 2 y 3. Progresivamente se hace más difícil. En este libro hay ocho lecciones y Pasatiempos. Cada lección trata de un tema común, por ejemplo: Un lugar donde vivir, Una visita al banco, etc. Los temas de las otras cuatro lecciones tratan sobre la historia y el gobierno de EE UU. Las lecciones están presentadas en inglés y traducidas al español. Todas las instrucciones están en español. Los Pasatiempos incluyen crucigramas, acertijos, y busca palabras. Al final del libro hay dos diccionarios: Inglés - Español y Español-Inglés; y un índice.

Cada lección está dividida en varias partes. Primero, hay una lista del vocabulario. En la lista se incluyen palabras básicas del inglés, así como el vocabulario del tema en particular. Después hay una conversación para usar el vocabulario en tal situación. Luego hay una historia relacionada al tema que refuerza el vocabulario y la conversación. La página número cuatro de cada lección es un ejercicio que requiere que el alumno elija una palabra de la lista del vocabulario y entonces que el alumno escriba la palabra en una oración en que falta una palabra. Las próximas tres páginas son una variedad de páginas con actividades. Al fin de cada lección están las respuestas de los ejercicios para ayudar al alumno a tener éxito.

Se sugiere que el estudiante haga una lección cada semana, pero el alumno puede pasar por el libro más rápidamente si así lo desea. La rapidez con la cual el alumno vaya a aprender inglés depende del alumno mismo. Será muy útil leer en voz alta la conversación y la historia. Eso ayudará al estudiante a obtener fluidez. El estudiante debe utilizar todo el tiempo un buen should

check the phonetic pronunciation of new words. The pupil should continually add his own new words to his notebook.

Also, the student should listen to television in English. In the beginning the pupil should listen to ads, cartoons, and news. The student should be familiar with the news in Spanish. It is very important to listen to and speak with English speakers. That will help the student greatly. He or she will be able to practice his or her English and also improve his or her accent. No one is ever going to learn English without practice. Children learn quickly to speak English. The reason for this is that most children are not bothered by the mistakes they make in speaking. It is important to take advantage of every opportunity to speak.

The student should keep Books 1, 2, 3 and 4. These will be valuable reference materials.

Good Luck!

diccionario: Español-inglés; Inglés-español. Sin falta el estudiante debe comprobar la pronunciación de las palabras nuevas en el diccionario. El alumno debe poner sus propias palabras nuevas en su cuaderno.

También, el alumno debe escuchar la televisión en inglés. En el principio ayuda escuchar los anuncios, las caricaturas, y las noticias si es que el estudiante ya sabe las noticias en español. Es muy importante hablar con y escuchar a personas que hablan inglés. Eso ayudará al alumno muchísimo con la práctica y el acento. Nunca se va a aprender inglés sin la práctica. Los niños aprenden muy rápidamente a hablar inglés. La razón por la cual es que a la mayoría de los niños no les importa las equivocaciones al hablar. Es importante aprovechar cualquier oportunidad que tengan para hablar inglés.

El estudiante debe conservar los Libros 1, 2, 3 y 4. Serán muy valiosos como materia de consulta.

¡Buena Suerte!

NOTES

Lesson 1 The Post Office
Lección 1 La oficina postal

Vocabulary List   Lista de Vocabulario

1. stamps	1. estampillas
2. to mail	2. enviar
3. package	3. paquete
4. envelope	4. sobre
5. letter	5. carta
6. to weigh	6. pesar
7. first class	7. primera clase
8. roll	8. rollo
9. book	9. libro
10. to collect	10. coleccionar
11. design	11. diseño
12. collection	12. colección

Conversation

1. I am going to the post office to buy stamps. Do you want me to mail your package to Aunt Thelma? (Maria)

2. Yes, please. They will weigh the package at the post office and tell you how much the postage will be. (Catalina)

3. Hello. I would like to buy some stamps. (M)

4. Would you like to buy a book or a roll of stamps? (mail clerk)

5. How many stamps are in a book? (M)

6. We have books of 15 or 20 stamps. (mc)

7. How many stamps are in a roll? (M)

8. A hundred stamps are in a roll. (mc)

9. I will buy a roll of stamps. (M)

10. You can also buy stamps by mail or by phone and that way you do not need to stand in line or come to the post office. (mc)

11. Thank you. I also need to mail this package. (M)

Conversación

1. Voy a la oficina postal a comprar estampillas. ¿Quieres que envíe tu paquete para tía Thelma? (María)

2. Sí por favor. En la oficina postal pesarán el paquete y te indicarán el porte que debes pagar. (Catalina)

3. Hola. Me gustaría comprar algunas estampillas. (M)

4. ¿Le gustaría comprar un libro o un rollo de estampillas? (empleado postal)

5. ¿Cuántas estampillas hay en un libro? (M)

6. Tenemos libros de 15 o 20 estampillas. (ep)

7. ¿Cuántas estampillas hay en un rollo? (M)

8. Hay cien estampillas en un rollo. (ep)

9. Compraré un rollo de estampillas. (M)

10. También puede comprar estampillas por correo o por teléfono y así no necesita hacer fila ni venir a la oficina postal. (ep)

11. Gracias. También necesito enviar este paquete. (M)

Story

The Post Office

For his birthday, Enrique received a box of playing cards from his grandparents. The gift came in the mail. On the package were several first class stamps that he will add to his stamp collection. Enrique has just finished writing a thank you letter to his grandparents. Next he will address the envelope. He learned in school where to put the destination and return addresses. After lunch, Jose is taking Enrique to the post office. Enrique enjoys picking out a first class stamp with a special subject or interest design on it. He and his grandfather both have stamp collections. His grandfather has stamps from all over the world and many are very old. Most of Enrique's stamps are from the United States. Enrique keeps his stamps in a beautifully bound album.

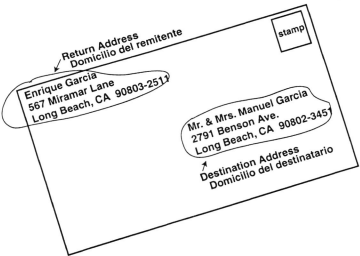

Historia

La oficina postal

Para su cumpleaños, Enrique recibió una caja de naipes que le enviaron sus abuelos. El regalo le llegó por correo. En el paquete había varias estampillas de primera clase que Enrique añadió a su colección de estampillas. Enrique acaba de escribir una carta de agradecimiento para sus abuelos. Luego escribirá el domicilio en el sobre. En la escuela aprendió dónde poner el domicilio del destinatario y el del remitente. Después del almuerzo, José va a llevar a Enrique a la oficina postal. Enrique disfruta escogiendo una estampilla de primera clase con un tema especial o diseño de interés. Él y su abuelo tienen colecciones de estampillas. Su abuelo tiene estampillas de todo el mundo y muchas son muy antiguas. La mayoría de las estampillas de Enrique son de Estados Unidos. Enrique guarda sus estampillas en un álbum bellamente encuadernado.

Fill in the Blank * Llene el Espacio

Llene cada espacio con una palabra de la lista del vocabulario. Use cada palabra solamente una vez.

1. Enrique writes his return address on the _____ .

2. A hundred stamps are in a _____ .

3. Enrique keeps his _____ in a beautifully bound album.

4. You can buy _____ by mail.

5. Enrique's package had several _____ stamps on it.

6. Catalina has a _____ to mail to Aunt Thelma.

7. Maria offered to _____ the package.

8. Many people like to _____ stamps.

9. Did you write a thank you _____ to your grandparents?

10. I am going to buy the stamps with the new _____ for Christmas.

11. They need to _____ the package to tell how much the postage will be.

12. Do you want a _____ or a roll of stamps?

The Gerund * El gerundio

El gerundio es la forma *ing* (ando, endo) de los verbos. Si el verbo termina con una consonante y la letra "e", se le quita la "e" antes de añadirle la terminación "ing". Si el verbo tiene una vocal y una consonante, entonces se repite la consonante antes de añadir "ing".

Escriba el gerundio de los siguientes verbos. Hicimos los tres primeros como ejemplo.

1. brush	*brushing*	16. drink	
2. vote	voting	17. earn	
3. bat	batting	18. get	
4. buy		19. go	
5. bring		20. give	
6. bid		21. help	
7. collect		22. learn	
8. pay		23. have	
9. call		24. weigh	
10. celebrate		25. live	
11. take		26. graduate	
12. cook		27. sleep	
13. decide		28. practice	
14. write		29. run	
15. do		30. study	

Days of the Week * Días de la Semana

Español	Inglés
domingo	Sunday
lunes	Monday
martes	Tuesday
miércoles	Wednesday
jueves	Thursday
viernes	Friday
sábado	Saturday

En inglés los días de la semana se escriben en letras mayúsculas y no se usa el artículo.

Escriba las oraciones siguientes en inglés.

1. Los martes Enrique trabaja después la escuela.

_____

2. Los viernes mi familia va al cine.

_____

3. El domingo José va a la iglesia.

_____

4. Catalina juega fútbol los miércoles.

_____

5. El sábado los niños miran las caricaturas en la televisión.

_____

6. El lunes mi abuela va al doctor.

_____

7. Los jueves María visita su mamá.

_____

Past Progressive Tense
Tiempo pasado progresivo

El tiempo pasado progresivo indica una acción que se realizó en el pasado. Por ejemplo: *Yesterday I was walking home when it began to rain: Ayer estaba caminando a mi casa cuando empezó a llover.*

Escriba las oraciones siguientes en inglés.

1. Después de la escuela ella estaba jugando con sus amigas.

   _____

2. Antes de trabajar mi madre estaba limpiando la casa.

   _____

3. Estábamos viendo el juego de béisbol.

   _____

4. Anoche los niños estaban haciendo la tarea.

   _____

5. Estabas visitando a tu hija la semana pasada.

   _____

6. Estaba ayudando a la maestra después del almuerzo.

   _____

7. Mi hermano estaba hablando por teléfono durante veinte minutos.

   _____

8. Estaba lloviendo cuando regresé a casa.

   _____

Answer Key * Las Respuestas

Fill in the Blank * Llene el Espacio (page 4)
1. envelope
2. roll
3. collection
4. stamps
5. first class
6. package
7. mail
8. collect
9. letter
10. design
11. weigh
12. book

The Gerund * El gerundio (page 5)

1.	brushing	11.	taking	21.	helping
2.	voting	12.	cooking	22.	learning
3.	batting	13.	deciding	23.	having
4.	buying	14.	writing	24.	weighing
5.	bringing	15.	doing	25.	living
6.	bidding	16.	drinking	26.	graduating
7.	collecting	17.	earning	27.	sleeping
8.	paying	18.	getting	28.	practicing
9.	calling	19.	going	29.	running
10.	celebrating	20.	giving	30.	studying

Days of the Week * Días de la Semana (page 6)
1. On Tuesdays Enrique works after school.
2. On Fridays my family goes to the movies.
3. On Sunday Jose goes to church.
4. Catalina plays soccer on Wednesdays.
5. On Saturday the children watch cartoons on television.
6. On Monday my grandmother goes to the doctor.
7. On Tuesdays Maria visits her mother.

Past Progressive Tense * Tiempo pasado progresivo (page 7)
1. After school she was playing with her friends.
2. Before work, my mother was cleaning the house.
3. We were watching the baseball game.
4. Last night the children were doing homework.
5. You were visiting your daughter last weekend.
6. I was helping the teacher after lunch.
7. My brother was talking on the telephone for twenty minutes.
8. It was raining when we came home.

Lesson 2 The American Revolution
Lección 2 La Revolución Americana

Vocabulary List

1. colonies
2. to refuse
3. war
4. why?
5. taxes
6. to sign
7. independence
8. debts
9. colonists
10. to pay
11. troops
12. colonial

Lista de Vocabulario

1. colonias
2. negarse
3. guerra
4. ¿por qué?
5. impuestos
6. firmar
7. independencia
8. deudas
9. colonizadores
10. pagar
11. tropas
12. colonial

Conversation

1. Tonight we will discuss the American Revolution. How many colonies were there before the War of Independence? (teacher)

2. There were thirteen colonies. They were founded by settlers from England between 1607 and 1732. (student)

3. Why were the colonists upset with their parent country, England? (t)

4. In 1765, England began imposing taxes without consulting the colonial governments. (s)

5. What did the colonists do? (t)

6. They refused to pay these taxes. (s)

7. What did England do? (t)

8. England sent soldiers to force the colonists to pay taxes. War broke out in 1775. (s)

9. Why did England impose these taxes upon the colonists? (t)

10. England had many debts. It needed money to help pay the cost of maintaining troops in its colonies. (s)

Conversación

1. Esta noche hablaremos sobre la Revolución Americana. ¿Cuántas colonias había antes de la Guerra de Independencia? (maestro)

2. Había trece colonias. Los colonizadores provenientes de Inglaterra las fundaron entre 1607 y 1732. (estudiante)

3. ¿Por qué los colonizadores se disgustaron con Inglaterra, su país de origen? (m)

4. En 1765, Inglaterra comenzó a cobrar impuestos sin consultar con los gobiernos de las colonias. (e)

5. ¿Qué hicieron los colonizadores? (m)

6. Se negaron a pagar estos impuestos. (e)

7. ¿Qué hizo Inglaterra? (m)

8. Inglaterra envió soldados para forzar a los colonizadores a pagar impuestos. La guerra comenzó en 1775. (e)

9. ¿Por qué Inglaterra impuso estos impuestos a los colonizadores? (m)

10. Inglaterra tenía muchas deudas. Necesitaba dinero para pagar el costo del mantenimiento de las tropas en sus colonias. (e)

Story

The American Revolution

The American Revolution was a war between the thirteen English colonies in North America and their parent country, England. The war lasted from 1775 to 1783. In 1775, England sent troops to force the colonists to pay taxes. The war began in Massachusetts in April 1775. On July 4, 1776, the colonial delegates adopted the Declaration of Independence. During this session of Congress, the members appointed George Washington as commander in chief of all the colonial armies. They issued paper money and established local governments. There were many battles in the fight for Independence. Finally, in September 1783, a peace treaty was signed in Paris. America had won its independence from England! In 1787, delegates from the newly formed republic met in Philadelphia, Pennsylvania to write the Constitution. This Constitution gave extensive powers to the central government, especially in the areas of economics and war, and also gave power to the individual states.

Historia

La Revolución Americana

La Revolución Americana fue una guerra entre las trece colonias inglesas de Norteamérica y su país de origen, Inglaterra. La guerra duró de 1775 a 1783. En 1775, Inglaterra envió tropas para forzar a los colonizadores a pagar impuestos. La guerra comenzó en Massachusetts en abril de 1775. El 4 de julio de 1776, los delegados coloniales adoptaron la Declaración de Independencia. Durante esta sesión del Congreso, los miembros nombraron a George Washington comandante en jefe de todo el ejército de las colonias. Emitieron billetes y establecieron gobiernos locales. Hubo muchas batallas en la lucha por la independencia. Finalmente, en septiembre de 1783, se firmó un tratado de paz en París. ¡Las colonias americanas habían ganado su independencia de Inglaterra! En 1787, los delegados de la recién formada república se reunieron en Filadelfia, Pennsylvania para redactar la Constitución. Esta Constitución otorgó extensos poderes al gobierno central, especialmente en las áreas de economía y guerra, y también otorgó poderes a los estados individuales.

Fill in the Blank * Llene el Espacio

Llene cada espacio con una palabra de la lista del vocabulario. Use cada palabra solamente una vez.

1. The _____ refused to pay the unfair taxes.

2. England had many _____ from maintaining its colonies.

3. _____ were the colonists upset?

4. The colonists _____ to pay the taxes.

5. In 1783, they went to Paris to _____ a peace treaty.

6. There were thirteen _____ .

7. The colonists had to _____ high taxes on tea.

8. The _____ began in Massachusetts.

9. England sent _____ to force the colonists to pay taxes.

10. England imposed _____ on the colonies.

11. America won its _____ from England.

12. The _____ leaders adopted the Declaration of Independence.

Future Tense Using "Go" + Infinitive
Tiempo futuro usando "go" (ir) + infinitivo

Este tiempo futuro expresa una acción que se va a realizar en el futuro.

Español	Inglés
voy + infinitivo*	I am going + infinitive*
vas + infinitivo	you are going + infinitive
va + infinitivo	(he, she, it) is going + infinitive
vamos + infinitivo	we are going + infinitive
vais + infinitivo	you (plural) are going + infinitive
van + infinitivo	they are going + infinitive

*El infinitivo es la forma simple del verbo con la palabra "to" al principio. Algunos ejemplos de infinitivo son: to come (venir), to go (ir), to study (estudiar), etc.

Escriba las siguientes oraciones en tiempo futuro. La primera ya está hecha.

1. Martha va a visitar a su abuela esta tarde.

   Martha is going to visit her grandmother this afternoon.

2. Voy a ir de compras el sábado.

   _____

3. Vamos a estudiar a la biblioteca esta noche.

   _____

4. Ellos van a comprar un auto nuevo el próximo año.

   _____

5. Ana va a comenzar una colección de estampillas cuando cumpla diez años.

   _____

6. Thelma va a rentar un apartamento cerca de la escuela donde trabaja.

   _____

7. Va a llover esta tarde.

   _____

8. Vas a cenar en un restaurante.

   _____

Months of the Year * Los meses del año

Español	Inglés
enero	January
febrero	February
marzo	March
abril	April
mayo	May
junio	June
julio	July
agosto	August
septiembre	September
octubre	October
noviembre	November
diciembre	December

En inglés las meses del año se escriben en letras mayúsculas.

Escriba las oraciones siguientes en inglés.

1. El día de San Valentín es en febrero.

   _____

2. Visitamos a nuestros abuelos en noviembre.

   _____

3. Mis meses favoritos del año son junio, julio y agosto.

   _____

4. La escuela comienza en septiembre.

   _____

5. En mayo vamos a ir de vacaciones a México.

   _____

6. Mi cita con el médico fue en marzo.

   _____

7. En diciembre, enero y febrero el clima es frío.

   _____

8. Los cumpleaños de mis hermanas son en octubre y abril.

   _____

14

Hard and Soft "C" * La "c" dura y suave

En inglés la "c" tiene dos sonidos: uno duro y uno suave. Si la "c" está antes de las letras "a", "o", "u" o de una consonante, entonces tiene un sonido duro como la letra "k". Si la "c" está antes de la "e", "i" o la "y", tiene un sonido suave como la letra "s".

Pronuncie las siguientes palabras y luego escriba "soft" (suave) o "hard" (dura) dependiendo del sonido que haga la "c". La primera ya está hecha.

1. car	*hard*	16. applications	
2. cat		17. voice	
3. pencil		18. cold	
4. carrot		19. medicine	
5. collar		20. clock	
6. ice		21. mice	
7. executive		22. celebrate	
8. dance		23. officer	
9. call		24. groceries	
10. celebrate		25. collect	
11. bacon		26. recess	
12. cook		27. cloudy	
13. decide		28. coin	
14. color		29. coke	
15. city		30. excessive	

Answer Key * Las Respuestas

Fill in the Blank * Llene el Espacio (page 12)

1. colonists
2. debts
3. Why
4. refused
5. sign
6. colonies
7. pay
8. war
9. troops
10. taxes
11. independence
12. colonial

Future Tense * Tiempo futuro (page 13)

1. Marta is going to visit her grandmother this afternoon.
2. I am going to go shopping on Saturday.
3. We are going to study at the library this evening.
4. They are going to buy a new car next year.
5. Ana is going to start a stamp collection when she is ten years old.
6. Thelma is going to rent an apartment near the school where she works.
7. It is going to rain this afternoon.
8. You are going to eat at a restaurant for dinner.

Months of the Year * Los meses del año (page 14)

1. Valentine's Day is in February.
2. We visited our grandparents in November.
3. June, July, and August are my favorite months of the year.
4. School begins in September.
5. In May, we are going on vacation to Mexico.
6. My appointment with the doctor was in March.
7. In December, January, and February, the weather is cold.
8. My sisters' birthdays are in October and April.

Hard and Soft "C" * La "c" dura y suave * (page 15)

1.	hard	11.	hard	21.	soft
2.	hard	12.	hard	22.	soft
3.	soft	13.	soft	23.	soft
4.	hard	14.	hard	24.	soft
5.	hard	15.	soft	25.	hard
6.	soft	16.	hard	26.	soft
7.	hard	17.	soft	27.	hard
8.	soft	18.	hard	28.	hard
9.	hard	19.	soft	29.	hard
10.	soft	20.	hard	30.	soft

Lesson 3 A Place to Live
Lección 3 Un lugar donde vivir

Vocabulary List	Lista de Vocabulario
1. apartment	1. apartamento
2. furnished	2. amueblado
3. to rent	3. rentar
4. available	4. vacante
5. loan	5. préstamo
6. bid	6. oferta
7. pool	7. piscina
8. backyard	8. patio
9. security deposit	9. depósito de seguridad
10. realtor	10. agente de bienes raíces
11. garage	11. garage
12. down payment	12. enganche

Conversation

1. Hello. I want to rent an apartment. (Thelma)

2. What size of an apartment are you looking for? (manager)

3. I am looking for a furnished one bedroom apartment. (T)

4. We have a couple of furnished one bedroom apartments available and several studios. (m)

5. What is a studio? (T)

6. A studio is smaller. Ours have one large room, a kitchen, and a bathroom. They are less expensive than the one bedroom apartments. (m)

7. I will look at both styles. Is there a pool? (T)

8. Yes, we have a pool, two Jacuzzis, and an exercise room. Would you like an apartment with or without a fireplace? (m)

9. I do not want a fireplace. (T)

10. We require a security deposit and the first month's rent before you can move in. Please follow me and I will show you the apartments. (m)

Conversación

1. Hola, deseo rentar un apartamento. (Thelma)

2. ¿Qué tamaño de apartamento desea? (gerente)

3. Estoy buscando un apartamento amueblado de una recámara. (T)

4. Tenemos un par de apartamentos amueblados de una recámara y varios estudios. (g)

5. ¿Qué es un estudio? (T)

6. Un estudio es más pequeño. Los nuestros tienen una habitación grande, una cocina y un baño. Son más económicos que un apartamento de una recámara. (g)

7. Veré ambos estilos. ¿Hay una piscina? (T)

8. Sí, tenemos una piscina, dos *Jacuzzis* y una sala para ejercicios. ¿Le gustaría un apartamento con o sin chimenea? (g)

9. No quiero chimenea. (T)

10. Necesitamos un depósito de seguridad y el primer mes de renta antes de que se mude. Por favor sígame y le mostraré los apartamentos. (g)

Story

Buying a House

Luz and Jose are planning to buy a new house. They need a larger home for their family. They want their new house to be near a good school for their children. They also want it near a public library and located in a city that has a good recreational program. They are looking for a four bedroom house with a two car garage. They also want a large backyard for the children and dog. Jose and Luz talk to a realtor. They let the realtor know what they want. The realtor shows them several houses. After many weeks of looking, they find one they like. They bid on the house. Their bid is accepted. They pay a down payment and wait for their loan to be approved. Finally, their loan is approved. They are told what their monthly payments will be. Jose and Luz's family is excited about moving into their new home and neighborhood.

Historia

La compra de una casa

Luz y José planean comprar una casa nueva. Necesitan una casa más grande para su familia. Quieren que la casa nueva quede cerca de una buena escuela para sus hijos. También quieren que quede cerca de una biblioteca pública y que esté en una ciudad que cuente con un buen programa de actividades recreativas. Están buscando una casa con cuatro recámaras y garage para dos autos. También desean que el patio sea grande para los niños y el perro. José y Luz hablan con un agente de bienes raíces. Le dicen lo que desean. El agente les muestra varias casas. Después de varias semanas de búsqueda encuentran una que les gusta. Presentan una oferta por la casa. Se acepta su oferta. Pagan un enganche y esperan que el préstamo se apruebe. Finalmente el préstamo se aprueba. Les indican la cantidad de los pagos mensuales. La familia de José y Luz están entusiasmado sobre la mudanza a su nueva casa y a su nuevo vecindario.

Fill in the Blank * Llene el Espacio

Llene cada espacio con una palabra de la lista del vocabulario. Use cada palabra solamente una vez.

1. There is a heated _____ and two Jacuzzis.

2. I plan to get my _____ back when I move out.

3. Are you going to look for a house to _____ or to buy?

4. It will take a month before the _____ is approved.

5. Luz and Jose saved money every month for their _____ .

6. She does not want an _____ with a fireplace.

7. The _____ shows them several houses.

8. After choosing a house, Luz and Jose have to _____ on it.

9. This apartment is _____ with a refrigerator, stove, and bed.

10. Will you have a _____ for your car?

11. We will have several apartments _____ next month.

12. My dog needs a big _____ to run in.

Future Tense Using the Auxiliary Verb *Will*
Tiempo futuro usando el verbo auxiliar *will*

El tiempo futuro expresa una acción que se realizará en el futuro.

Pronombre	Verbo
I, you, he, she, it, we, they	will + la forma simple del verbo*

*En inglés no se escribe "to" después de "will". Use la forma simple del verbo y no el infinitivo, por ejemplo: come (venir), go (ir), study (estudiar), etc.

Escriba las siguientes oraciones en tiempo futuro. La primera ya está hecha.

1. Iré al banco mañana en la mañana.

   I will go to the bank tomorrow morning.

2. María y los niños almorzarán en McDonald's.

   _____

3. Los niños beberán refrescos fríos en el picnic del sábado.

   _____

4. Este verano manejaré a California para visitar a nuestros abuelos.

   _____

5. Costará mucho dinero ir a la universidad.

   _____

6. Después de la escuela Enrique leerá su libro en la biblioteca.

   _____

7. Dormirás en casa de la abuela la noche del viernes.

   _____

8. Nos pondremos nuestros vestidos amarillos nuevos para la fiesta de cumpleaños.

   _____

Vocabulary Practice * Práctica de vocabulario

Encuentre el significado de cada palabra. Escriba el número que corresponde al significado enfrente de cada palabra. La primera ya está hecha.

__8__	medicine	1. a job
	street	2. a group of rooms a person rents
	boot	3. different kinds of food that are for sale
	coupon	4. a drink made of ice cream, milk and flavoring, shaken up or mixed
	warm	5. a short coat
	cloudy	6. the area behind a house
	apartment	7. road
	coach	8. pills or liquids that make sick people feel better
	groceries	9. a certificate for a discount or refund
	milkshake	10. a covering for the foot that is made of leather or rubber and is worn to keep the foot dry and warm
	work	11. having clouds in the sky
	field	12. a meeting where a person asks questions of one or more other people
	jacket	13. a covering for the hand that has a separate place for each finger
	interview	14. a person who teaches or trains someone in sports, acting, or singing
	backyard	15. between hot and cool
	gloves	16. before the usual time
	early	17. a piece of land that has no woods or buildings
	sunny	18. having a lot of sunshine

22

Hard and Soft "G" * La "g" dura y suave

La "g" tiene dos sonidos: uno duro y uno suave. Si la "g" está antes de las letras "a", "o", "u" o de una consonante, entonces tiene un sonido duro como la "g" de "go". Si la "g" está antes de las letras "e", "i", o "y", entonces generalmente tiene un sonido suave como la "g" de "orange". Hay algunas excepciones como las palabras "give", "get" y "girl".

Pronuncie las siguientes palabras y luego escriba "soft" (suave) o "hard" (duro) dependiendo del sonido que haga la "g". La primera ya está hecha.

1. big	*hard*	16. legislative	
2. game		17. glad	
3. flag		18. Thanksgiving	
4. large		19. goes	
5. dog		20. gun	
6. package		21. grape	
7. bring		22. emergency	
8. gas		23. delegates	
9. goal		24. England	
10. leg		25. groceries	
11. good		26. pig	
12. age		27. goat	
13. egg		28. sponge	
14. green		29. giraffe	
15. bag		30. stage	

Answer Key * Las Respuestas

Fill in the Blank * Llene el Espacio (page 20)

1. pool
2. security deposit
3. rent
4. loan
5. down payment
6. apartment
7. realtor
8. bid
9. furnished
10. garage
11. available
12. backyard

Future Tense * Tiempo futuro (page 21)

1. I will go to the bank tomorrow morning.
2. Maria and the children will eat at a McDonald's for lunch.
3. The children will drink cold sodas at the picnic on Saturday.
4. This summer we will drive to California to visit our grandparents.
5. It will cost a lot of money to go to college.
6. After school, Enrique will read his book at the library.
7. You will sleep at grandma's house on Friday night.
8. We will wear our new yellow dresses to the birthday party.

Vocabulary Practice * Práctica de vocabulario (page 22)

1. 8	7. 2	13. 5
2. 7	8. 14	14. 12
3. 10	9. 3	15. 6
4. 9	10. 4	16. 13
5. 15	11. 1	17. 16
6. 11	12. 17	18. 18

Hard and Soft "G" * La "g" dura y suave * (page 23)

1. hard	11. hard	21. hard
2. hard	12. soft	22. soft
3. hard	13. hard	23. hard
4. soft	14. hard	24. hard
5. hard	15. hard	25. hard
6. soft	16. soft	26. hard
7. hard	17. hard	27. hard
8. hard	18. hard	28. soft
9. hard	19. hard	29. soft
10. hard	20. hard	30. soft

Lesson 4 The President
Lección 4 El presidente

Vocabulary List
Lista de Vocabulario

1. service
2. to unify
3. convention
4. army
5. to resign
6. first
7. to win
8. amendment
9. to serve
10. twice
11. leader
12. eldest

1. servicio
2. unificar
3. convención
4. ejército
5. renunciar
6. primero
7. ganar
8. enmienda
9. servir
10. dos veces
11. líder
12. mayor

Conversation

1. Tonight in class we are going to discuss the executive branch of the government. Who is in charge of the executive branch? (teacher)

2. The president of the United States of America is in charge of the executive branch. (student)

3. If the president should die who would take his/her place? (t)

4. The vice president would become president. (s)

5. How many terms can a president serve? (t)

6. The president can serve two terms. (s)

7. How many years are in a term for the office of president? (t)

8. A term is four years. (s)

9. Has a president ever served more than two terms? (t)

10. Yes, President Franklin D. Roosevelt served four terms, but in 1951 the 22nd Amendment to the Constitution stated "no person shall be elected President more than twice." (s)

Conversación

1. Esta noche en clase vamos a hablar sobre la rama ejecutiva del gobierno. ¿Quién está a cargo de la rama ejecutiva? (maestro)

2. El presidente de Estados Unidos de América está encargado de la rama ejecutiva. (estudiante)

3. Si el presidente muriese, ¿quién tomaría su lugar? (m)

4. El vicepresidente se convertiría en presidente. (e)

5. ¿Cuántos mandatos puede servir el presidente? (m)

6. El presidente puede servir dos mandatos. (e)

7. ¿Cuántos años tiene el mandato para el cargo de presidente? (m)

8. El mandato tiene cuatro años. (e)

9. ¿Algún presidente ha servido por más de dos mandatos? (m)

10. Sí, el presidente Franklin D. Roosevelt sirvió cuatro mandatos, pero en 1951 la 22ava. Enmienda a la Constitución dispuso que "ninguna persona deberá ser electa más de dos veces para el cargo de presidente." (e)

Story

Presidents of the United States

George Washington was the first president of the United States of America. He helped the American colonies win their freedom from England and then played a large role in helping to unify the new states. He was the eldest son of a well-to-do Virginia farmer. During the American Revolution, George Washington was the Commander in Chief of the Continental Army. After the war, he was chosen president of the Constitutional Convention. Because of his service in America's fight for independence and his participation in helping to unify the states, George Washington was elected the country's first president. He served for two terms. George Washington is known as "The Father of Our Country." Abraham Lincoln, Franklin D. Roosevelt, and John F. Kennedy are other well-known presidents. Several presidents died during their term of office and one president resigned.

Historia

Los presidentes de Estados Unidos

George Washington fue el primer presidente de Estados Unidos de América. Washington ayudó a que las colonias americanas ganaran su libertad de Inglaterra y luego desempeñó un papel muy importante en la unificación de los nuevos estados. Washington era el hijo mayor de un próspero granjero de Virginia. Durante la Revolución Americana, George Washington era el comandante en jefe del Ejército Continental. Después de la guerra fue elegido presidente de la Convención Constitucional. Debido a su servicio en la lucha de Estados Unidos por su independencia y su participación en la unificación de los estados, George Washington fue elegido el primer presidente del país. Sirvió dos mandatos. George Washington es conocido como el "Padre de nuestro país". Abraham Lincoln, Franklin D. Roosevelt y John F. Kennedy son otros presidentes muy famosos. Varios presidentes murieron durante su mandato y un presidente renunció.

Fill in the Blank * Llene el Espacio

Llene cada espacio con una palabra de la lista del vocabulario. Use cada palabra solamente una vez.

1. A person my be elected president _____ .

2. What can you do to _____ your country?

3. The colonists formed an _____ to fight for independence.

4. Because of his _____ in the fight for independence, George Washington was elected president.

5. He played a role in helping to _____ the new states.

6. George was the _____ son of a Virginia farmer.

7. Washington was chosen president of the Constitutional _____ .

8. The _____ made a change to the Constitution.

9. Who is the _____ of the executive branch?

10. Instead of facing impeachment, the president decided to _____ .

11. Who do you want to _____ the election?

12. George Washington was the _____ president of the United States.

Sentence Practice * Práctica con Oraciones

Escriba las oraciones siguientes en inglés.

1. Mañana iré a nadar con mis amigos.

   _____

2. Estuvimos en la escuela hasta las cuatro.

   _____

3. Mi madre estaba visitando a mis abuelos la semana
   pasada.

   _____

4. El próximo mes mi padre se va de viaje.

   _____

5. La semana pasada conociste a mi nuevo amigo.

   _____

6. El sábado nuestros abuelos vinieron a casa a cenar.

   _____

7. El viernes mis hermanas y yo vimos una buena
   película.

   _____

8. El domingo las niñas fueron a una fiesta.

   _____

9. El miércoles los niños visitaron el museo.

   _____

Plural * Plural

Usualmente para formar el plural en inglés se añade una "s" al final de la palabra. Si la palabra termina en "s", "ch", "sh", o "x" hay que añadir "es". Si la palabra termina en "y" con una consonante enfrente hay que cambiar la "y" por una "i" y hay que añadir "es". Si la palabra termina en "f" o "fe", cambie la "f" o "fe" por una "v" y añada "es".

Escriba el plural de las palabras abajo.

1. address	_____	16. birthday	_____
2. brother	_____	17. family	_____
3. colony	_____	18. woman	_____
4. blouse	_____	19. house	_____
5. collar	_____	20. idea	_____
6. banana	_____	21. leash	_____
7. man	_____	22. package	_____
8. dress	_____	23. puppy	_____
9. emergency	_____	24. straw	_____
10. army	_____	25. child	_____
11. mouse	_____	26. tax	_____
12. baby	_____	27. test	_____
13. watch	_____	28. knife	_____
14. leader	_____	29. six	_____
15. branch	_____	30. wife	_____

Vocabulary Practice * Práctica de vocabulario

Encuentre el significado de cada palabra. Escriba el número que corresponde al significado enfrente de cada palabra. La primera ya está hecha.

__16__ baseball	1. a sauce made from tomatoes that gives flavor to foods	
_____ package	2. ready to use or have	
_____ loan	3. the cost to join a club or to buy a service	
_____ season	4. stopping work or play for a short time	
_____ recess	5. oldest	
_____ amendment	6. what a person does to make a living	
_____ ketchup	7. to have furniture	
_____ eldest	8. a piece of paper that a person uses to give information when asking for a job	
_____ individual	9. something that is owed	
_____ available	10. a special day	
_____ beer	11. a change in or addition to something	
_____ application	12. an alcoholic drink made of malt and water, and flavored with hops	
_____ furnished	13. a brown drink made from the beans of a coffee plant	
_____ coffee	14. a time of the year that has a certain kind of weather	
_____ debt	15. money or something that must be repaid or returned	
_____ holiday	16. a game that two teams play with a bat and ball	
_____ career	17. a box with things inside that is wrapped with paper	
_____ fee	18. one person	

Answer Key * Las Respuestas

Fill in the Blank * Llene el Espacio (page 28)

1. twice
2. serve
3. army
4. service
5. unify
6. eldest
7. Convention
8. amendment
9. leader
10. resign
11. win
12. first

Sentence Practice * Práctica con Oraciones (page 29)

1. Tomorrow, I will go swimming with my friends.
2. We were at school until four o'clock.
3. My mother was visiting my grandparents last week.
4. Next month, my father is going on a trip.
5. Last week, you met my new friend.
6. On Saturday, our grandparents came to our house for dinner.
7. My sisters and I saw a good movie on Friday.
8. The girls went to the party on Sunday.
9. The children will visit the museum on Wednesday.

Plural * Plural (page 30)

1. addresses	11. mice	21. leashes
2. brothers	12. babies	22. packages
3. colonies	13. watches	23. puppies
4. blouses	14. leaders	24. straws
5. collars	15. branches	25. children
6. bananas	16. birthdays	26. taxes
7. men	17. families	27. tests
8. dresses	18. women	28. knives
9. emergencies	19. houses	29. sixes
10. armies	20. ideas	30. wives

Vocabulary Practice * Práctica de vocabulario (page 31)

1. 16	7. 1	13. 7
2. 17	8. 5	14. 13
3. 15	9. 18	15. 9
4. 14	10. 2	16. 10
5. 4	11. 12	17. 6
6. 11	12. 8	18. 3

Lesson 5 Emergencies
Lección 5 Emergencias

Vocabulary List

1. to help
2. bottle
3. kitchen
4. to call
5. poison control
6. counter
7. behavior
8. to watch
9. couple
10. emergency
11. rescue
12. crew

Lista de Vocabulario

1. ayudar
2. frasco
3. cocina
4. llamar
5. centro de control de envenenamientos
6. gabinete
7. conducta
8. observar
9. dos
10. emergencia
11. rescate
12. equipo

Conversation

1. Mother, Peter drank the bottle of medicine. (Catalina)

2. What do you mean? (Maria)

3. Someone must have left the bottle of medicine on the counter with the top off. When I came into the kitchen, Peter was drinking it. (C)

4. I will call poison control. (M)

5. Poison control. May I help you? (agent)

6. Yes, my son just drank a bottle of medicine. (M)

7. What kind of medicine? (a)

8. It was Amoxicillin. (M)

9. How much did your son drink? (a)

10. It looks like he drank about a fourth of a bottle. (M)

11. He will probably vomit soon. (a)

12. Is there anything I can do? (M)

13. Yes, watch your son for the next couple of hours. If you notice any unusual behavior, please call back. (a)

14. Thank you for your help. (M)

Conversación

1. Mamá, Pedro se bebió el frasco de medicina. (Catalina)

2. ¿Qué quieres decir? (María)

3. Alguien dejó el frasco de medicina abierto en el gabinete. Cuando entré a la cocina Pedro se la estaba bebiendo. (C)

4. Llamaré al centro de control de envenenamientos. (M)

5. Centro de control de envenenamientos. ¿Puedo ayudarle? (agente)

6. Sí, mi hijo acaba de beber un frasco de medicina. (M)

7. ¿Qué clase de medicina? (a)

8. Era amoxicilina. (M)

9. ¿Cuánta medicina bebió su hijo? (a)

10. Parece que bebió aproximadamente un cuarto del frasco. (M)

11. Probablemente vomitará muy pronto. (a)

12. ¿Hay algo que pueda hacer? (M)

13. Sí, observe a su hijo durante las próximas dos horas. Si nota una conducta rara, por favor vuelva a llamarnos. (a)

14. Gracias por su ayuda. (M)

Story

Calling 911

Enrique came home from school and found his grandmother sitting in a chair. She would not wake up. Enrique was scared. He called 911. "Emergency Services. What's your emergency?"

"My grandmother will not wake up. I came home from school and found her sitting in her chair. I tried to wake her up."

"What is the address where you are?"

"I am at my grandmother's house. Her address is 845 Park Lane, Long Beach."

"A rescue crew will be there in five to ten minutes."

"Thank you." Enrique went back to the living room where his grandmother was sitting. He held his grandmother's hand until the rescue crew arrived.

Historia

Llamadas de emergencia al 911

Enrique regresó a casa de la escuela y encontró a su abuelita sentada en una silla. No la pudo despertar. Enrique se asustó. Llamó al 911. "Servicio de emergencia. ¿Cuál es su emergencia?"

"Mi abuela no despierta. Regresé a casa de la escuela y la encontré sentada en una silla. Traté de despertarla."

"¿Cuál es su dirección?"

"Estoy en casa de mi abuela. Su dirección es el 845 Park Lane, Long Beach."

"Un equipo de rescate estará ahí de cinco a diez minutos."

"Gracias." Enrique regresó a la sala donde estaba sentada su abuela. Tomó la mano de su abuelita hasta que llegó el equipo de rescate.

Fill in the Blank * Llene el Espacio

Llene cada espacio con una palabra de la lista del vocabulario. Use cada palabra solamente una vez.

1. Enrique is going to _____ for the rescue team to arrive.

2. His grandmother will be fine in a _____ of days.

3. Catalina went into the _____ for something to eat.

4. A _____ is a team of people.

5. _____ is dangerous or deadly.

6. Watch for unusual _____ .

7. Call _____ if you suspect someone touched, drank, or ate poison.

8. There is a _____ of medicine in the bathroom cabinet.

9. The _____ crew arrived in five minutes.

10. Thank you for your _____ .

11. Try to stay calm in an _____ .

12. Do you know the emergency number to _____ for help?

Expressing Ability * Expresión de habilidad

Use el verbo auxiliar *can (poder)* + el verbo principal para expresar habilidad y posibilidad. Por ejemplo: *I can speak English: Yo puedo hablar inglés. Can (puedo)* es el verbo auxiliar y *speak (hablar)* es el verbo principal (main verb).

Pronoun	Verb
I, you, he, she, it, we, they	can + main verb*

*No use "to" después de "can". Use la forma simple del verbo y no el infinitivo, por ejemplo: wear (ponerse), help (ayudar), play (jugar), etc.

Escriba las oraciones siguientes en inglés.

1. Las niñas pueden ponerse sus vestidos azules el domingo.

   _____

2. Puedo llamarte a las ocho de la mañana.

   _____

3. El médico puede examinar a su hijo a las cuatro de esta tarde.

   _____

4. Podemos almorzar con nuestros amigos.

   _____

5. Puedes alimentar al perro después de la cena.

   _____

6. Mamá y yo podemos ayudar a la abuela el sábado.

   _____

7. Puedes enviar este paquete en la oficina postal.

   _____

8. Los niños pueden jugar en el parque después de la escuela.

   _____

Vocabulary Practice * Práctica de vocabulario

Encuentre el significado de cada palabra. Escriba el número que corresponde al significado enfrente de cada palabra. La primera ya está hecha.

__11__ leader	1. to give aid
_____ rescue	2. to do something again and again to improve
_____ uniform	3. two times
_____ team	4. the water that falls out of the clouds
_____ sugar	5. to have a party or ceremony
_____ tax	6. not old
_____ umbrella	7. a small, sticky piece of paper that is put on a letter or package to show that the cost of mailing has been paid
_____ stamp	8. cloth or plastic that is stretched over a folding frame, held up by a stick, and used to protect a person from rain or sun
_____ twice	9. having a lot of air moving
_____ practice	10. to save from danger or harm
_____ thirsty	11. a person who guides other people
_____ help	12. needing water
_____ windy	13. clothes of a special kind that are worn by all the people who are members of a certain group
_____ skirt	14. a piece of paper or cloth that a person uses to clean the face and hands while eating
_____ celebrate	15. a group of people who work together for the same goal
_____ rain	16. a piece of clothing that hangs below the waist
_____ young	17. a white, grainy substance that tastes sweet
_____ napkin	18. money people must pay to the government

Practice with Contractions
Práctica con contracciones

Completa las oraciones con las palabras de la casilla.

I'm	isn't	that's	you're
didn't	she's	let's	don't
he's	it's	I'll	doesn't

1. _____ go swimming after church.

2. My friend _____ going to the party on Saturday.

3. _____ going to do your homework now.

4. _____ doing her homework right now.

5. Where is the ball? _____ under the table.

6. My sister _____ go to school today.

7. Enrique _____ go to Catalina's school.

8. They _____ have any milk for their lunch.

9. _____ going to my grandma's house after school.

10. _____ a very good student.

11. Tomorrow _____ go shopping with mother.

12. _____ a very good answer!

Answer Key * Las Respuestas

Fill in the Blank * Llene el Espacio (page 36)

1. watch
2. couple
3. kitchen
4. crew
5. Poison
6. behavior
7. poison control
8. bottle
9. rescue
10. help
11. emergency
12. call

Expressing Ability * Expresión de habilidad (page 37)

1. The girls can wear their blue dresses on Sunday.
2. I can call you at eight o'clock in the morning.
3. The doctor can examine your son at four o'clock this afternoon.
4. We can eat lunch with our friends.
5. We can feed the dog after dinner.
6. Mother and I can help grandma on Saturday.
7. You can mail this package at the post office.
8. The children can play in the park after school.

Vocabulary Practice * Práctica de vocabulario (page 38)

1. 11	7. 8	13. 9
2. 10	8. 7	14. 16
3. 13	9. 3	15. 5
4. 15	10. 2	16. 4
5. 17	11. 12	17. 6
6. 18	12. 1	18. 14

Practice with Contractions * Práctica con contracciones (page 39)

1. Let's
2. isn't
3. You're
4. She's
5. It's
6. didn't
7. doesn't
8. don't
9. I'm
10. He's
11. I'll
12. That's

Lesson 6 The Constitution
Lección 6 La Constitución

Vocabulary List

1. to govern
2. weak
3. delegates
4. document
5. to write
6. basic
7. supreme
8. Constitution
9. individual
10. to decide
11. rights
12. too

Lista de Vocabulario

1. gobernar
2. débil
3. delegados
4. documento
5. escribir
6. básica
7. suprema
8. Constitución
9. individuo
10. decidir
11. derechos
12. también

Conversation

1. Tonight, students, we are going to discuss the Constitution of the United States. The Constitution became effective in 1789 and contains the basic laws of the United States of America. Can there be changes to the Constitution? (teacher)

2. Yes, these changes or additions are called Amendments. (student)

3. What are the first 10 Amendments to the Constitution called? (t)

4. They are called the Bill of Rights. (s)

5. When were these 10 Amendments ratified? (t)

6. They were ratified in December 1791. (s)

7. Why is the Bill of Rights so important? (t)

8. It safeguards the individual's rights against excess authority by the central government. (s)

9. Who can list some of these rights? (t)

10. Freedom of speech, freedom of religion, freedom of press, and freedom to assemble peacefully are some of the rights provided in the Bill of Rights. (s)

Conversación

1. Estudiantes, esta noche vamos a hablar sobre la Constitución de Estados Unidos. La Constitución entró en vigencia en 1789 y contiene las leyes básicas de Estados Unidos de América. ¿Pueden hacerse cambios a la Constitución? (maestro)

2. Sí, estos cambios o adiciones se llaman enmiendas. (estudiante)

3. ¿Cómo se les llama a las primeras diez enmiendas de la Constitución? (m)

4. Se les llama Declaración de Derechos. (e)

5. ¿Cuándo se ratificaron estas diez enmiendas? (m)

6. Se ratificaron en diciembre de 1791. (e)

7. ¿Por qué es tan importante la Declaración de Derechos? (m)

8. Es la protección de los derechos de los individuos contra el exceso de autoridad del gobierno central. (e)

9. ¿Quién puede decir algunos de esos derechos? (m)

10. La libertad de expresión, la libertad de religión, la libertad de prensa, y la libertad de reunirse pacíficamente, son algunos de los derechos que contiene la Declaración de Derechos. (e)

Story

The Constitution of the United States

The Articles of Confederation was the first constitution of the United States. The Articles of Confederation became the basic law for the new republic between 1781 and 1788. Under these Articles, the central government was too weak to govern the thirteen states. In 1787, delegates from the different states met at the Constitutional Convention in Philadelphia to write a new document. They needed to decide how to divide power between the central government and the states. The delegates decided to give extensive power to the central government, but reserved many powers to the states. The delegates decided to have three branches of government: legislative, judicial, and executive. This would allow for one branch of government to check or balance those of the other branches. The legislative branch would be divided into two houses: the Senate and the House of Representatives. Each state would have two senators and the number of representatives would depend on the number of people in each state. The Constitutional Convention was in session for 16 weeks. This new Constitution which became effective in 1789 has remained the supreme law of the United States for over 200 years.

Historia

La Constitución de Estados Unidos

Los Artículos de la Confederación fue la primera constitución de Estados Unidos. Los Artículos de la Confederación se convirtieron en la ley básica de la nueva república entre 1781 y 1788. Bajo estos artículos el gobierno central era muy débil para gobernar los trece estados. En 1787, los delegados de los diferentes estados se reunieron en la Convención Constitucional que se celebró en Filadelfia para escribir un nuevo documento. Necesitaban decidir cómo dividir el poder entre el gobierno central y los estados. Los delegados decidieron otorgar poder extenso al gobierno central, pero reservaron muchos poderes para los estados. Los delegados decidieron formar tres ramas de gobierno: legislativo, judicial y ejecutivo. Esto permitiría que una rama del gobierno revisara o equilibrara los poderes de las otras ramas. La rama legislativa se dividiría en dos cámaras: el Senado y la Cámara de Representantes. Cada estado tendría dos senadores y el número de representantes dependería del número de habitantes de cada estado. La Convención Constitucional estuvo en sesión durante 16 semanas. Esta nueva constitución, que entró en vigencia en 1789, ha sido la ley suprema de Estados durante más de 200 años.

Fill in the Blank * Llene el Espacio

Llene cada espacio con una palabra de la lista del vocabulario. Use cada palabra solamente una vez.

1. The _____ met in Philadelphia.

2. They met to _____ a new Constitution.

3. Three branches share power to _____ the United States.

4. One branch should not have _____ much power over the other two.

5. The Bill of Rights safeguards the _____ rights.

6. Under the Articles of Confederation, the central government was too_____ .

7. A new _____ was written at the Constitutional Convention.

8. The _____ became effective in 1789.

9. The Constitution has remained the _____ law for over 200 years.

10. It contains the _____ laws of the United States.

11. Who can list the _____ provided by the first 10 amendments?

12. The delegates met to _____ how to divide power.

Expressing Ability in the Past Tense
Expresión de habilidad en tiempo pasado

Use el verbo auxiliar *could (podía)* + el verbo principal para expresar habilidad y posibilidad en el pasado. Por ejemplo, *I could ride my bike when I was four years old. Podía andar en bicicleta cuando tenía cuatro años. Could (podía)* es el verbo auxiliar y *ride (andar)* es el verbo principal (main verb).

Pronoun	Verb
I, you, he, she, it, we, they	could + main verb*

*No use "to" después de "could". Use la forma simple del verbo, no el infinitivo.

Escriba las oraciones siguientes en inglés.

1. Cuando visité a mi tía podía ir a la playa todos los días.

_____

2. Ayer pudimos ir a nadar. Hoy hace mucho frío.

_____

3. Esta tarde mi amigo pudo batear la pelota muy lejos.

_____

La contracción de "can not" es "can't" y de "could not" es "couldn't". Escriba las siguientes oraciones usando estas contracciones.

4. No puedes ir a la fiesta el viernes.

_____

5. No pudieron visitar a su madre el verano pasado.

_____

6. No pude ir al cine anoche.

_____

7. No puedo votar porque soy muy joven.

_____

Homonyms * Homónimos

Un homónimo es una palabra que se pronuncia igual a otra pero que tiene diferente significado y se escribe diferente.

Relacione las palabras de la derecha con su homónimo. La primera ya está hecha.

				blew
1. eight	<u>ate</u>	13. red	_____	ate
				to
2. eye	_____	14. mail	_____	for
				bored
3. two	_____	15. hair	_____	here
				I
4. no	_____	16. four	_____	hare
				new
5. buy	_____	17. meat	_____	know
				knight
6. week	_____	18. board	_____	our
				dew
7. write	_____	19. sale	_____	male
				weak
8. road	_____	20. piece	_____	right
				peace
9. night	_____	21. do	_____	sail
				rode
10. hear	_____	22. blue	_____	dye
				role
11. hour	_____	23. knew	_____	by
				read
12. roll	_____	24. die	_____	meet

Sentence Practice * Práctica con Oraciones

Escriba las oraciones siguientes en inglés.

1. Anoche estaba estudiando en casa de mi amigo.

    _____

2. Vamos a ir al banco esta tarde.

    _____

3. Los niños caminaron a casa desde la escuela.

    _____

4. Necesitaba cinco dólares para comprar una chaqueta.

    _____

5. Regalaron un auto nuevo a su padre por su
    cumpleaños.

    _____

6. Te sentaste en la silla de mi padre.

    _____

7. Limpiaremos la casa el sábado.

    _____

8. Ella no puede encontrar sus llaves.

    _____

9. Renté un apartamento grande cerca de la escuela.

    _____

Answer Key * Las Respuestas

Fill in the Blank * Llene el Espacio (page 44)

1. delegates
2. write
3. govern
4. too
5. individual's
6. weak
7. document
8. Constitution
9. supreme
10. basic
11. rights
12. decide

Expressing Ability in the Past Tense * Expresión de habilidad en tiempo pasado (page 45)

1. When I visited my aunt, I could go to the beach everyday.
2. Yesterday we could go swimming. Today it is too cold.
3. This afternoon my friend could bat the ball far.
4. You can't go to the party on Friday.
5. They couldn't visit their mother last summer.
6. I couldn't go to the movies last night.
7. I can't vote because I'm too young.

Homonyms * Homónimos (page 46)

1. ate	7. right	13. read	19. sail
2. I	8. rode	14. male	20. peace
3. to	9. knight	15. hare	21. dew
4. know	10. here	16. for	22. blew
5. by	11. our	17. meet	23. new
6. weak	12. role	18. bored	24. dye

Sentence Practice * Práctica con Oraciones (page 47)

1. I was studying at my friend's house last night.
2. We will be going to the bank this afternoon.
3. The children walked home from school.
4. He needed five dollars to buy the jacket.
5. They gave their father a new car for his birthday.
6. You sat in my father's chair.
7. We will clean the house on Saturday.
8. She can't find her keys.
9. I rented a large apartment near the school.

Lesson 7 A Visit to the Bank
Lección 7 Una visita al banco

Vocabulary List	Lista de Vocabulario
1. money	1. dinero
2. savings account	2. cuenta de ahorros
3. checking account	3. cuenta de cheques
4. to open	4. abrir
5. social security number	5. número de seguro social
6. to transfer	6. transferir
7. interest	7. interés
8. fee	8. tarifa
9. minimum balance	9. balance mínimo
10. to deposit	10. depositar
11. checks	11. cheques
12. service charge	12. cargo por servicio

Conversation

1. Hello. I want to open a checking account. (Thelma)
2. Thank you for selecting our bank. (bank clerk)
3. I have $500 to deposit into my new checking account. (T)
4. There is no monthly service charge if you keep the minimum balance in your checking account. Please look through this book and pick out the design for your checks. (bc)
5. How soon will my new checks and checkbook arrive? (T)
6. They will arrive in three weeks. Until then you can use these temporary checks. What information do you want on your checks? (bc)
7. I want my name and address on my checks. How can I deposit money into my account? (T)
8. You can send it by mail, use the ATM (automatic teller machine), or come into the bank. (bc)
9. I will deposit my paycheck by mail. Thank you for your help. (T)
10. Thank you. The bank appreciates your business. (bc)

Conversación

1. Hola, deseo abrir una cuenta de cheques. (Thelma)
2. Gracias por escoger nuestro banco. (empleado del banco)
3. Tengo $500 para depositar en mi nueva cuenta de cheques. (T)
4. No hay cargo mensual por servicio si mantiene un balance mínimo en su cuenta de cheques. Por favor revise este libro y escoja un diseño para sus cheques. (edb)
5. ¿Cuándo llegarán mi chequera y cheques nuevos? (T)
6. Llegarán en tres semanas. Mientras tanto puede usar estos cheques temporales. ¿Qué información desea que pongamos en sus cheques? (edb)
7. Quiero que pongan mi nombre y domicilio en mis cheques. ¿Cómo puedo depositar dinero en mi cuenta? (T)
8. Puede enviarlo por correo, usar la ATM (máquina cajera automática), o venir al banco. (edb)
9. Depositaré el cheque de mi sueldo por correo. Gracias por su ayuda. (T)
10. Gracias a usted. El banco agradece su negocio. (edb)

Story

Opening a Savings Account

Maria and Miguel go to the bank to open a savings account for their children's college education. They speak with a bank clerk. They want to open their savings account with $500. The bank clerk asks for their social security numbers. They plan to deposit $200 a month into this savings account. They will use the ATM to make their deposits. They already have ATM cards. Their monthly bank statement will show how much money is in their savings account and how much interest they have earned. With this savings account there is no monthly fee and no minimum balance. If they need to transfer money from this account to their checking account, they can do so. But Maria and Miguel plan not to use this money until their children go to college.

Historia

Apertura de una cuenta de ahorros

María y Miguel van al banco a abrir una cuenta de ahorros para la educación universitaria de sus hijos. Hablan con un empleado del banco. Desean abrir su cuenta de ahorros con $500. El empleado del banco les pregunta sus números de seguro social. Planean depositar $200 al mes en esta cuenta de ahorros. Usarán la ATM para hacer los depósitos. Ya tienen tarjetas para la ATM. Su estado bancario mensual mostrará cuánto dinero tienen en su cuenta de ahorros y cuánto interés han ganado. En esta cuenta de ahorros no se cobran tarifas mensuales ni se necesita un balance mínimo. Pueden transferir dinero desde esta cuenta a su cuenta de cheques si lo necesitan. Pero María y Miguel planean no usar este dinero sino hasta que sus hijos vayan a la universidad.

Fill in the Blank * Llene el Espacio

Llene cada espacio con una palabra de la lista del vocabulario. Use cada palabra solamente una vez.

1. Are you going to _____ a savings or checking account?

2. He is going to _____ $100 from his checking account to his savings account.

3. There will be a _____ if the minimum balance is below $1000.

4. Thelma wants to open a _____ .

5. Maria and Miguel open a _____ .

6. This account has no fee or _____ .

7. My _____ is 710-22-0000.

8. The _____ for that account will be billed monthly.

9. How much _____ does that account earn in a year?

10. Would you like to order _____ with the flower design?

11. _____ your check in the slot provided.

12. Two hundred years ago, most people did not keep _____ in a bank.

Writing the Date * Cómo escribir la fecha

Escriba las siguientes fechas poniendo el nombre del mes seguido de los números del día y del año. El nombre del mes se comienza con mayúscula y se escribe una coma después del día. La primera ya está hecha.

1. 3/27/09   March 27, 2009

2. 5/8/08

3. 1/17/01

4. 8/7/52

5. 6/23/98

6. 2/1/02

7. 11/13/10

8. 4/14/89

9. 7/6/00

10. 12/22/09

11. 10/11/87

12. 9/3/03

13. 4/8/11

14. 7/4/12

Writing Dollars and Cents on a Check
Cómo escribir dólares y centavos en un cheque

Escriba la cantidad en dólares y centavos como lo haría en un cheque. En inglés se escribe un guión después de veinte, treinta, cuarenta, cincuenta, sesenta, setenta, ochenta y noventa cuando se escriben números como del veintiuno al veintinueve. Hicimos los dos primeros como ejemplo.

1. $24.58	Twenty-four and 58/100
2. $342.77	Three hundred forty-two and 77/100
3. $108.50	
4. $515.25	
5. $432.08	
6. $83.37	
7. $47.12	
8. $78.46	
9. $57.99	
10. $61.49	
11. $129.59	
12. $212.34	
13. $99.99	
14. $854.37	

Writing a Check
Cómo escribir un cheque

Complete el cheque siguiendo las instrucciones.

```
CAROLINA AND MIGUEL MARTINEZ                    ①              415
        725 PARK STREET                   DATE _____
     LONG BEACH, CA  90806-2055

PAY TO THE    ②                               ③
ORDER OF_____    $ [_____]

   ④
_____  D O L L A R S


FIRST NATIONAL BANK
916 MAGNOLIA AVENUE                       ⑤
LONG BEACH, CA  90807-3217                   _____

   1223945 ':3789:' 10339:' 09832
```

Directions:

Pretend you are Carolina or Miguel and you have just bought a washing machine from Sears. The machine cost $729.99

1. Fill in the date. You can make up your own day.

2. Write the name of the company to whom the check is payable.

3. Write the amount of the check in numbers.

4.   Write the amount of the check in words.

5. Sign the check.

Instrucciones:

Suponga que usted es Carolina o Miguel y que acaba de comprar una lavadora en Sears. La lavadora costó $729.99

1. Escriba la fecha. Puede inventarse una fecha.
2. Escriba el nombre de la compañía a quien se pagará el cheque.
3. Escriba la cantidad del cheque con números.
4. Escriba la cantidad del cheque con palabras.
5. Firme el cheque.

Answer Key * Las Respuestas

Fill in the Blank * Llene el Espacio (page 52)

1. open
2. transfer
3. fee
4. checking account
5. savings account
6. minimum balance
7. social security number
8. service charge
9. interest
10. checks
11. Deposit
12. money

Writing the Date * Cómo escribir la fecha (page 53)

1. March 27, 2000	6. February 1, 2002	11. October 11, 1987
2. May 8, 2008	7. November 13, 2010	12. September 3, 2008
3. January 17, 2001	8. April 14, 1989	13. April 8, 2011
4. August 7, 1952	9. July 6, 2000	14. July 4, 2012
5. June 23, 1998	10. December 22, 2009	

Writing Dollars and Cents on a Check * Cómo escribir dólares y centavos en un cheque (page 54)

1. Twenty-four and 58/100	8. Seventy-eight and 46/100
2. Three hundred forty-two and 77/100	9. Fifty-seven and 99/100
3. One hundred eight and 50/100	10. Sixty-one and 49/100
4. Five hundred fifteen and 25/100	11. One hundred twenty-nine and 59/100
5. Four hundred thirty-two and 8/100	12. Two hundred twelve and 34/100
6. Eighty-three and 37/100	13. Ninety-nine and 99/100
7. Forty-seven and 12/100	14. Eight hundred fifty-four and 37/100

Writing a Check * Cómo escribir un cheque (page 55)

CAROLINA AND MIGUEL MARTINEZ
725 PARK STREET
LONG BEACH, CA 90806-2055

① DATE January 15, 2009   415

PAY TO THE ② Sears
ORDER OF _____

③ $ 729.99

④ Seven hundred twenty-nine and 99/100   DOLLARS

FIRST NATIONAL BANK
916 MAGNOLIA AVENUE
LONG BEACH, CA 90807-3217

⑤ *Carolina Martinez*

1223945 ':3789:' 10339:' 09832

Lesson 8 Local & State Government
Lección 8 Los gobiernos local y estatal

Vocabulary List	Lista de Vocabulario
1. governor	1. gobernador
2. Democrat	2. demócrata
3. Republican	3. republicano
4. to register	4. registrarse
5. political	5. político
6. party	6. partido
7. meeting	7. reunión
8. member	8. miembro
9. to support	9. apoyar
10. to vote	10. votar
11. neighbor	11. vecino
12. community	12. comunidad

Conversation

1. Jose, don't forget to vote today. (Luz)

2. Where do I go to vote? (Jose)

3. Our polling place is at Westfield Park. (L)

4. Where at Westfield Park? (J)

5. It will be inside the recreation building. (L)

6. When can I go? (J)

7. You can vote between 7:00 a.m. and 7:00 p.m. (L)

8. I will stop on my way to work. (J)

9. I plan to vote at lunch time. (L)

10. Do I need to take anything? (J)

11. Bring some identification. You will need to sign the voter registration book before you can vote. (L)

12. I can't wait until I can vote. (Enrique)

13. You will have to wait until you're eighteen. (L)

14. What are you voting for today? (E)

15. We are voting for city council members. (L)

Conversación

1. José, que no se te olvide votar hoy. (Luz)

2. ¿Dónde debo votar? (José)

3. Nuestro lugar de votación es en Westfield Park. (L)

4. ¿Dónde en Westfield Park? (J)

5. Estará dentro del edificio de actividades recreativas. (L)

6. ¿Cuándo puedo ir? (J)

7. Puedes votar ente las 7:00 a.m. y las 7:00 p.m. (L)

8. Iré de camino al trabajo. (J)

9. Yo pienso votar a la hora del almuerzo. (L)

10. ¿Necesito llevar algo? (J)

11. Lleva alguna identificación. Necesitarás firmar el registro electoral antes de poder votar. (L)

12. No puedo esperar para votar. (Enrique)

13. Tendrás que esperar hasta que tengas dieciocho años. (L)

14. ¿Para qué vas a votar hoy? (E)

15. Vamos a votar para elegir a los miembros del concejo municipal. (L)

Story

Registered to Vote

When Luz registered to vote, she registered as a Democrat. Jose registered as a Republican. The Democrat and Republican parties are the two largest political parties in the United States. Luz and Jose have a neighbor who is a member of the state assembly. Their state legislature is made up of a 40 member Senate and an 80 member Assembly. Jose and Luz walked their precinct, handing out flyers in support of their neighbor when he ran for the state assembly. Jose and Luz are active members in their community. They often attend city council meetings because they like to know what decisions are being made about their town. In November, they will vote for governor. The governor is the state's chief executive. Even though Luz is registered as a Democrat and Jose as a Republican, they often vote for the same person. In November, they both plan to vote for the Democratic candidate for governor.

Historia

Registrado para votar

Cuando Luz se registró para votar, se registró como demócrata. José se registró como republicano. Los partidos demócrata y republicano son los dos partidos políticos más grandes de Estados Unidos. Luz y José tienen un vecino que es miembro de la asamblea estatal. Su legislatura estatal está constituida por un Senado de 40 miembros y una asamblea de 80 miembros. José y Luz recorrieron su precinto electoral repartiendo volantes para apoyar a su vecino cuando se presentó como candidato para la asamblea estatal. José y Luz son miembros activos de su comunidad. Frecuentemente asisten a reuniones del concejo municipal porque les gusta enterarse de las decisiones que se toman acerca de su ciudad. En noviembre votarán por un gobernador. El gobernador es el jefe ejecutivo del estado. Aunque Luz está registrada como demócrata y José como republicano, frecuentemente votan por la misma persona. En noviembre ambos piensan votar por el candidato demócrata para gobernador.

Fill in the Blank * Llene el Espacio

Llene cada espacio con una palabra de la lista del vocabulario. Use cada palabra solamente una vez.

1. Enrique must be eighteen to _____ to vote.

2. Luz is an active _____ in the community.

3. The _____ is the state's chief executive.

4. Important issues will be discussed at the _____ tonight.

5. Can I count on you to _____ our candidate?

6. Luz is a registered _____ .

7. Jose registered to vote as a _____ .

8. Which political _____ do you support?

9. She must do ten hours of _____ service for breaking the law.

10. Luz and Jose will _____ for governor at the next election.

11. Their _____ is a member of the state assembly.

12. What are the two largest _____ parties in the United States?

60

Sentence Practice * Práctica con Oraciones

Escriba las oraciones siguientes en inglés. Use contracciones cuando sea posible.

1. Mi abuela no pudo dormir anoche.

   _____

2. Compraste cinco camisas nuevas.

   _____

3. Dormimos en el patio la noche del viernes.

   _____

4. Nadé en el lago el sábado.

   _____

5. En el picnic bebieron refrescos y comieron hamburguesas.

   _____

6. Mi padre condujo su nuevo auto rojo al trabajo.

   _____

7. La familia llevó al perro en sus vacaciones.

   _____

8. Mi hermano no comenzará a ir a la escuela sino hasta octubre.

   _____

9. Compré comida, una cadena y un collar para mi perro.

   _____

More Practice with Contractions
Más práctica con contracciones

Contracción	Significado de la contracción
I'll	I will
you'll	you will
he'll, she'll, it'll	he will, she will, it will
we'll	we will
they'll	they will

La contracción de "will not" es "won't". Use contracciones cuando sea posible.

1. Ella depositará dinero en su cuenta de ahorros el viernes.

    _____

2. El sábado practicarán béisbol durante tres horas.

    _____

3. Rentaremos un apartamento grande cerca de la escuela de nuestros hijos.

    _____

4. Esta tarde enviaré esta carta en la oficina postal.

    _____

5. Este junio te graduarás de la universidad.

    _____

6. Ella no llamará sino hasta el domingo.

    _____

7. Verán el juego de fútbol soccer en la televisión.

    _____

8. "No me pondré la chaqueta amarilla," dijo Ana.

    _____

True or False * Verdadero o falso

Escriba una "T" si la frase es "true" o verdadero. Escriba una "F" si la frase es "false" o falso. Si la frase es falsa escriba en paréntesis la información para hacer que la oración sea verdadera. La primera ya está hecha.

__F__   1. There are 48 states in the United States of America. *(50 states)*

_____   2. The Congress makes the laws in the United States.

_____   3. The government of the United States has two branches.

_____   4. The first U.S. President was John F. Kennedy.

_____   5. The Declaration of Independence was adopted on December 25, 1942.

_____   6. The colors of the U.S. flag are red, white, and yellow.

_____   7. Congress meets in a building called the Capitol.

_____   8. The President of the United States is elected for a term of two years.

_____   9. The Pilgrims and Native Americans celebrated the first Memorial Day.

_____ 10. The Congress is the Senate and the House of Representatives.

_____ 11. There are fifty stars on the U.S. flag.

_____ 12. The Declaration of Independence is the supreme law of the United States.

_____ 13. The legislative branch is Congress.

_____ 14. The thirteen stripes on the U.S. flag represent the first thirteen Presidents of the United States.

_____ 15. You need to be 21 years old before you can vote.

_____ 16. The capital of the United States is New York City.

Answer Key * Las Respuestas

Fill in the Blank * Llene el Espacio (page 60)

1. register
2. member
3. governor
4. meeting
5. support
6. Democrat
7. Republican
8. party
9. community
10. vote
11. neighbor
12. political

Sentence Practice * Práctica con Oraciones (page 61)

1. My grandmother couldn't sleep last night.
2. You bought five new shirts.
3. We slept in the backyard on Friday night.
4. I swam at the lake on Saturday.
5. At the picnic, they drank sodas and ate hamburgers.
6. My father drove his new red car to work.
7. The family took their dog on vacation.
8. My brother won't start school until October.
9. I bought food, a leash, and a collar for my puppy.

More Practice with Contractions * Más practica con contracciones (page 62)

1. She'll deposit money in her savings account on Friday.
2. They'll practice baseball for three hours on Saturday.
3. We'll rent a large apartment near our children's school.
4. I'll mail this letter at the post office this afternoon.
5. You'll graduate from college this June.
6. She won't call until Sunday.
7. They'll watch the soccer game on television.
8. "I won't wear the yellow coat," said Ana.

True or False * Verdadero o falso (page 63)

1. F (50 states)
2. T
3. F (three)
4. F (George Washington)
5. F (July 4, 1776)
6. F (blue)
7. T
8. F (four)
9. F (Thanksgiving Day)
10. T
11. T
12. F (Constitution)
13. T
14. F (colonies)
15. F (eighteen)
16. F (Washington, D.C.)

PUZZLE FUN
PASATIEMPO

Crossword Puzzle * Crucigrama

Use las palabras contenidas en el vocabulario en inglés de las **Lecciones 1 & 2** para completar este crucigrama.

Across

2 pesar
6 coleccionar
8 independencia
12 estampillas
14 carta
16 colonizadores
18 tropas
19 guerra
20 primera clase
21 colonial

Down

1 colonias
3 por que
4 colección
5 libro
6 pagar
7 impuestos
9 diseño
10 deudas
11 sobre
13 paquete
15 rollo
17 enviar
18 firmar

Jumble * Mezcla de Palabras

Poner en orden las palabras del vocabulario de las Lecciones 1 & 2.

1. spoort _____

2. raw _____

3. signed _____

4. scoolien _____

5. ecnednepedni _____

6. amptss _____

7. obok _____

8. exast _____

9. bestd _____

10. gekaacp _____

11. locionsts _____

12. cellocnoti _____

13. levpeone _____

14. nicolalo _____

15. treelt _____

16. yhw _____

17. lrol _____

stamps
package
envelope
letter
roll
book
design
collection
colonies
war
why
taxes
independence
debts
colonists
troops
colonial

WordSearch * Busca Palabras

Encuentra las palabras de las **Lecciones 1 & 2** en el busca palabras. Marca las respuestas. Las palabras pueden estar escritas en forma normal, al revés o diagonalmente. El primer ejemplo está competo.

book	collection	colonial
colonies	colonists	debts
design	envelope	independence
letter	package	roll
stamps	taxes	troops
war	why	

C	E	W	W	D	C	F	N	A	S	P	O	O	R	T
O	N	K	S	A	E	O	F	G	J	P	Z	G	S	L
L	V	B	T	K	R	B	L	W	Y	J	W	I	L	W
O	E	H	A	L	C	A	T	L	N	K	N	O	H	R
N	L	I	M	I	D	K	H	S	E	D	R	Y	I	P
I	O	G	P	G	G	G	U	I	E	C	N	L	M	D
A	P	N	S	I	X	G	E	P	S	B	T	U	E	A
L	E	G	N	D	K	F	E	T	O	J	O	I	Y	L
Q	O	I	W	M	Z	N	S	S	S	P	U	O	O	G
S	N	S	O	O	D	I	E	Q	X	I	J	G	K	N
E	Y	E	W	E	N	X	O	X	W	P	E	L	M	P
Z	L	D	N	O	A	C	E	E	Q	K	H	X	E	K
V	H	C	L	T	L	E	T	T	E	R	F	U	B	S
N	E	O	G	F	I	F	Q	E	G	A	K	C	A	P
I	C	C	O	L	O	N	I	E	S	H	N	T	E	N

Crossword Puzzle * Crucigrama

Use las palabras contenidas en el vocabulario en inglés de las **Lecciones 3 & 4** para completar este crucigrama.

Across

1 renunciar
2 enganche
3 apartamento
6 patio
7 ejercito
9 deposito de seguridad
13 rentar
15 enmienda
16 mayor
19 vacante
22 amueblado

Down

1 unificar
4 primero
5 garage
8 piscina
9 servicio
10 convención
11 servir
12 dos veces
14 agente de bienes raíces
17 líder
18 ganar
20 préstamo
21 oferta

Jumble * Mezcla de Palabras

Poner en orden las palabras del vocabulario de las **Lecciones 3 & 4.**

1. onla _____
2. troaler _____
3. viceers _____
4. ritsf _____
5. metrapnta _____
6. tenconvion _____
7. steeld _____
8. yarm _____
9. edifrunsh _____
10. emdntnmea _____
11. redeal _____
12. viablelaa _____
13. drayackb _____
14. ragage _____
15. ewict _____
16. loop _____

apartment
furnished
available
loan
pool
backyard
realtor
garage
service
convention
army
first
amendment
twice
leader
eldest

70

WordSearch * Busca Palabras

Encuentra las palabras de las **Lecciones 3 & 4** en el busca palabras. Marca las respuestas. Las palabras pueden estar escritas en forma normal, al revés o diagonalmente. El primer ejemplo está competo.

amendment	apartment	army
available	backyard	convention
eldest	first	furnished
garage	leader	loan
pool	realtor	service
twice		

D	R	S	L	O	A	N	A	Q	H	T	I	S	P	R
G	R	M	E	G	S	M	D	X	B	M	Z	G	E	T
O	L	A	N	R	Y	V	P	T	O	O	D	D	S	G
E	P	W	Y	O	V	M	R	B	U	Z	A	E	Q	S
I	E	V	M	K	I	I	R	F	N	E	D	T	H	F
X	D	F	W	O	C	T	C	A	L	L	N	Y	H	Q
T	E	Y	C	W	A	A	N	E	E	E	B	K	P	N
N	H	H	S	T	H	N	B	E	M	K	T	O	G	C
E	S	B	M	R	H	T	R	D	V	F	K	F	N	V
M	I	A	B	F	W	O	N	H	G	N	I	K	Y	A
T	N	T	N	I	T	E	Y	E	M	A	O	R	G	J
R	R	L	C	L	M	P	T	W	L	L	R	C	S	N
A	U	E	A	A	F	N	Q	G	G	J	J	A	L	T
P	F	E	V	T	C	O	I	K	L	O	O	P	G	D
A	R	A	V	A	I	L	A	B	L	E	E	L	V	E

Crossword Puzzle * Crucigrama

Use las palabras contenidas en el vocabulario en inglés de las **Lecciones 5 & 6** para completar este crucigrama.

Across
3 conducta
5 derechos
6 observar
10 centro de control de envenenamientos
15 débil
16 frasco
19 cocina
20 documento
22 básica
23 emergencia
24 gobernar

Down
1 rescate
2 constitución
4 decidir
7 ayudar
8 individuo
9 escribir
11 suprema
12 equipo
13 también
14 dos
17 llamar
18 delegados
21 gabinete

Jumble * Mezcla de Palabras

Poner en orden las palabras del vocabulario de las Lecciones 5 & 6.

1. peocul _____	poison	
2. sreecu _____	bottle	
3. eakw _____	kitchen	
4. entdocum _____	behavior	
5. presume _____	couple	
6. stehealed _____	emergency	
7. duvinialid _____	rescue	
8. bletot _____	crew	
9. noittuitsCon _____	weak	
10. oto _____	delegates	
11. cymergene _____	document	
12. thigrs _____	excessive	
13. snoopi _____	supreme	
14. wrec _____	Constitution	
15. itchken _____	individual	
16. visesexec _____	rights	
17. havbreoi _____	too	

WordSearch * Busca Palabras

Encuentra las palabras de las **Lecciones 5 & 6** en el busca palabras. Marca las respuestas. Las palabras pueden estar escritas en forma normal, al revés o diagonalmente. El primer ejemplo está competo.

basic	behavior	bottle
Constitution	counter	couple
crew	document	emergency
individual	kitchen	rescue
supreme	too	weak

E	P	C	T	O	O	Q	N	X	U	M	D	B	C	B
D	L	R	R	F	J	P	G	F	K	C	A	O	A	W
O	C	T	C	E	N	V	D	N	V	W	U	S	T	E
C	N	Q	T	O	W	O	V	Q	I	P	I	S	D	A
U	V	R	C	O	N	Z	R	N	L	C	V	E	E	K
M	L	L	H	M	B	S	D	E	Q	G	E	I	P	X
E	W	Y	I	G	E	I	T	K	V	Y	K	B	I	X
N	H	H	G	P	V	C	S	I	I	K	R	L	J	O
T	W	D	Y	I	O	U	R	R	T	T	Y	S	B	Y
P	D	U	D	U	P	K	O	K	E	U	C	F	W	A
W	J	U	N	R	M	U	V	S	G	S	T	H	I	V
A	A	T	E	C	Y	X	Y	X	P	F	C	I	E	M
L	E	M	M	N	L	T	G	G	N	A	U	U	O	N
R	E	B	E	H	A	V	I	O	R	Y	G	V	E	N
E	M	E	R	G	E	N	C	Y	W	Z	X	H	S	V

74

Crossword Puzzle * Crucigrama

Use las palabras contenidas en el vocabulario en inglés de las **Lecciones 7 & 8** para completar este crucigrama.

Across

3 cuenta de ahorros
4 cuenta de cheques
6 interés
7 transferir
10 reunión
17 comunidad
18 partido
19 vecino
21 cargo por servicio

Down

1 gobernador
2 dinero
5 registrarse
8 político
9 depositar
10 balance mínimo
11 abrir
12 demócrata
13 republicano
14 apoyar
15 miembro
16 votar
17 cheques
20 tarifa

Jumble * Mezcla de Palabras

Poner en orden las palabras del vocabulario de las Lecciones 7 & 8.

1. vergoron_____	money
2. eef_____	savings
3. eoymn_____	checking
4. citalpoil_____	interest
5. remmbe_____	fee
6. broghein_____	checks
7. streetin_____	governor
8. licunco_____	Democrat
9. vingsas_____	Republican
10. giemnte_____	political
11. unitycomm_____	party
12. gnkicche_____	meeting
13. acnupRileb_____	member
14. sckech_____	council
15. trypa_____	neighbor
16. mocrateD_____	community

WordSearch * Busca Palabras

Encuentra las palabras de las **Lecciones 7 & 8** en el busca palabras. Marca las respuestas. Las palabras pueden estar escritas en forma normal, al revés o diagonalmente. El primer ejemplo está competo.

checks
democrat
interest
money
political

community
fee
meeting
neighbor
republican

council
governor
member
party

G	P	W	Q	L	K	N	B	Z	R	V	N	F	C	Y
G	N	A	J	V	P	G	D	L	J	Z	E	O	E	D
O	R	I	R	H	H	H	Q	V	A	E	U	N	O	E
V	U	E	T	T	N	D	K	H	S	N	O	T	A	M
E	Z	N	P	E	Y	F	U	C	C	M	V	G	K	O
R	S	F	F	U	E	F	T	I	C	F	F	X	R	C
N	Q	G	Y	Y	B	M	L	O	L	L	K	H	O	R
O	R	F	R	E	Y	L	M	V	E	B	K	H	B	A
R	Y	K	E	U	C	M	I	M	G	K	K	R	H	T
A	E	X	K	H	U	K	H	C	E	B	E	S	G	H
Y	R	Y	E	N	S	F	A	Y	A	M	Z	Q	I	Y
T	R	C	I	I	F	D	H	H	K	N	B	C	E	Z
I	K	T	V	A	R	X	J	L	O	Z	N	E	N	X
S	Y	F	F	I	T	S	E	R	E	T	N	I	R	D
S	Q	W	O	W	H	L	A	C	I	T	I	L	O	P

77

Answer Key * Las Respuestas

Crossword Puzzle * Crucigrama (page 66)

Across
2 to weigh
6 to collect
8 independence
12 stamps
14 letter
16 colonists
18 troops
19 war
20 first class
21 colonial

Down
1 colonies
3 why
4 collection
5 book
6 to pay
7 taxes
9 design
10 debts
11 envelope
13 package
15 roll
17 to mail
18 to sign

Jumble * Mezcla de Palabras (page 67)

1. troops
2. war
3. design
4. colonies
5. independence
6. stamps
7. book
8. taxes
9. debts
10. package
11. colonists
12. collection
13. envelope
14. colonial
15. letter
16. why
17. roll

WordSearch * Busca Palabras (page 68)

Crossword Puzzle * Crucigrama (page 69)

Across
1 to resign
2 down payment
3 apartment
6 backyard
7 army
9 security deposit
13 to rent
15 amendment
16 eldest
19 available
22 furnished

Down
1 to unify
4 first
5 garage
8 pool
9 service
10 convention
11 to serve
12 twice
14 realtor
17 leader
18 to win
20 loan
21 bid

78

Answer Key * Las Respuestas

Jumble * Mezcla de Palabras (page 70)

1. loan
2. realtor
3. service
4. first
5. apartment
6. convention
7. eldest
8. army
9. furnished
10. amendment
11. leader
12. available
13. backyard
14. garage
15. twice
16. pool

WordSearch * Busca Palabras (page 71)

Crossword Puzzle * Crucigrama (page 72)

Across

3 behavior
5 rights
6 to watch
10 poison control
15 weak
16 bottle
19 kitchen
20 document
22 basic
23 emergency
24 to govern

Down

1 rescue
2 constitution
4 to decide
7 to help
8 individual
9 to write
11 supreme
12 crew
13 too
14 couple
17 to call
18 delegates
21 counter

Jumble * Mezcla de Palabras (page 73)

1. couple
2. rescue
3. weak
4. document
5. supreme
6. delegates
7. individual
8. bottle
9. Constitution
10. too
11. emergency
12. rights
13. poison
14. crew
15. kitchen
16. excessive
17. behavior

Answer Key * Las Respuestas

WordSearch * Busca Palabras (page 74)

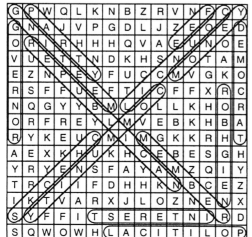

Crossword Puzzle * Crucigrama (page 75)

Across

3 savings account
4 checking account
6 interest
7 to transfer
10 meeting
17 community
18 party
19 neighbor
21 service charge

Down

1 governor
2 money
5 to register
8 political
9 to deposit
10 minimum balance
11 to open
12 democrat
13 republican
14 to support
15 member
16 to vote
17 checks
20 fee

Jumble * Mezcla de Palabras (page 76)

1. governor
2. fee
3. money
4. political
5. member
6. neighbor
7. interest
8. council
9. savings
10. meeting
11. community
12. checking
13. Republican
14. checks
15. party
16. Democrat

WordSearch * Busca Palabras (page 77)

Dictionary * Diccionario

English - Spanish * Inglés - Español

A

a - un, una
about - casi
action - acción
address - dirección
adjective - adjetivo
after - después
afternoon - tarde
airplane - avión
album - álbum
all - todo
also - también
always - siempre; todo el tiempo
American - americano
an - un, una
and - y
answer - respuesta
any - alguno; ninguno
anything - alguna cosa
apostrophe - apóstrofe
apple - manzana
appointment - cita
art - arte
as - como
at - en
ate - pasado de comer

B

baby - bebé
bacon - tocino
ball - pelota
banana - plátano
baseball - béisbol
bathing suit - traje de baño

be (to) - ser ; estar
   I am - soy; estoy
   you are - eres, es; estás, está
   he, she, it is - es; está
   we are - somos; estamos
   you (plural) are - sois; estáis
   they are - son; están
beach - playa
because - porque
bed - cama
bedroom - recámara
beer - cerveza
before - antes
behave (to) - portarse
bell - campana
belong to (to) - pertenecer
better - mejor
big - grande
black - negro
blacker - más negro
blackest - el más negro
blank - espacio
blouse - blusa
blue - azul
bluer - más azul
bluest - el más azul
board (blackboard) - pizarrón
boat - barco
body - cuerpo
book - libro
boy - muchacho
box - caja
bread - pan
breakfast - desayuno
bring (to) - llevar; traer
brother - hermano

brown - café
browner - más café
brownest - el más café
brush (to) - cepillar
building - edificio
bus - autobús
but - pero
buy (to) - comprar
    buying - comprando
by - por

C

California - un estado de los
    Estados Unidos
call (to) - llamar
    call roll (to) - pasar lista
capital - capital
car - carro
card - tarjeta
carefully - con cuidado
carrot - zanahoria
cartoons - caricaturas
cat - gato
celebrate (to) - celebrar
change - cambio
check - cheque
checkbook - chequera
chicken - pollo
child - niño
children - niños
chocolate - chocolate
church - iglesia
clean - limpio
cleaner - más limpio
cleanest - el más limpio
clock - reloj
clothes - ropa
coffee - café
cold - catarro; frio
colder - más frío

coldest - el más frío
colonists - colonos
color - color
come (to) - venir; llegar
contraction - contracción
conversation - conversación
cost (to) - costar
country - país
coupon - cupón
cream - crema
    ice cream - helado
cup - taza

D

date - fecha
daughter - hija
day - día
decide (to) - decidir
declare (to) - declarar
degree - grado
delicious - delicioso
department - departamento
    Department of Motor Vehicles -
    Departamento de Vehículos
    Motorizados
    DMV - Departamento de
    Vehículos Motorizados
depend (to) - depender
did (auxiliary) - verbo auxiliar
    usado con otros verbos para
    indicar el tiempo pasado,
    particularmente en las frases
    interrogativas y negativas;
    pasado de "hacer"
didn't [did not] - una contracción de
    "did not"
die (to) - morir
difficult - difícil
dime - una moneda de diez
    centavos

dinner - cena
direct - directo
dirty - sucio
do (to) - hacer
   I do - hago
   you do - haces; hace
   he, she, it does - hace
   we do - hacemos
   you (plural) do - hacéis
   they do - hacen
   doing - haciendo
doctor - doctor
doesn't [does not] - una contracción
   de "does not"
dog - perro
dollar - dólar
don't [do not] - una contracción de
   "do not"
Dr. - una abreviatura de doctor
drank - pasado de beber
dress - vestido
drink (to) - beber, tomar
drive (to) - manejar; conducir
driver - conductor
   driver's license - licencia de
   manejar
drove - pasado de manejar
during - durante

E

each - cada
ear - oído
early - temprano
eat (to) - comer
   I eat - como
   you eat - comes; come
   she, he, it eats - come
   we eat - comemos
   you (plural) eat - coméis
   they eat - comen

eating - comiendo
egg - huevo
eight - ocho
either - tampoco
English - inglés; inglesa
etc. - viene del latín et cetera que
   quiere decir "lo que se sigue"
every - cada
everything - todo
exam - examen
examine (to) - examinar
excellent - excelente
executes - ejecuta
expensive - costoso
eye - ojo

F

F - Fahrenheit refiere a la escala
   termométrica que se usa en los
   Estados Unidos
factory - fábrica
family - familia
favorite - favorito
feel (to) - sentirse
fever - fiebre
field - campo
fifty - cincuenta
fill out (to) - llenar
fine - fino
finer - más fino
finest - el más fino
fireplace - chimenea
first - primero
fish - pescado
five - cinco
flour - harina
flu - influenza
food -comida
foot - pie
for - por; para

found (to) - fundar
four - cuatro
fox - zorro
Friday - viernes
friend - amigo
from - de
fruit - fruta

G

gallon - galón
game - juego
gas station - gasolinera
gasoline - gasolina
gave - pasado de dar
geese - gansos
get (to) - obtener
get up (to) - subirse; levantarse
girl - muchacha
give (to) - dar
   giving - dando
go (to) - ir
   I go - voy
   you go - vas; va
   he, she, it goes - va
   we go - vamos
   you (plural) go - vais
   they go - van
   going - yendo
God - Dios
good - bueno
   good morning - buenos días
goose - ganso
government - gobierno
grade - grado
grape - uva
green - verde
greener - más verde
greenest - el más verde
groceries - abarrotes
grocery store - tienda de abarrotes

grow (to) - cultivar

H

had - pasado de tener
hair - pelo
half - mitad
hamburger - hamburguesa
hand - mano
handbook - manual
happy - feliz
hat - sombrero
have (to) - tener
   I have - tengo
   you have - tienes; tiene
   she, he, it has - tiene
   we have - tenemos
   you (plural) have - tenéis
   they have - tienen
have to (to) - tener que
he - él
he's [he is] - una contracción de "he is" que quiere decir "él es" o "él está"
help - ayuda
help (to) - ayudar
her - su, sus [de ella]
here - aquí
here's [here is] - una contracción de "here is" que quiere decir "aquí está"
hi! - ¡hola!
high - alto
higher - más alto
highest - el más alto
him - le, lo, o con él
himself - él mismo
his - su, sus [de él]
history - historia
hit (to) - pegar
holiday - día de fiesta

home - casa
homework - tarea
hotel - hotel
hour - hora
house - casa
how? - ¿cómo?
  how many? - ¿cuántos?
  how much? - ¿cuánto?
hungry – tener hambre
hurry (to) - apurarse

I

I - yo
I'll [I will] - una contracción de "I will" que quiere decir "yo haré"
I'm [I am] - una contracción de "I am" que quiere decir "yo soy" o "yo estoy"
ice cream - helado
if - si
in - en
interesting - interesante
interprets - interpreta
isn't [is not] - una contracción de "is not" que quiere decir "no es" o "no está"
it - ello
its - de ello
it's [it is] - una contracción de "it is" que quiere decir "ello es"

J

jacket - chaqueta
join - juntarse
jumprope - cuerda para brincar

K

key - llave
kiss - beso
know (to) - saber

L

law - ley
learn (to) - aprender
lesson - lección
let's [let us] - una contracción de "let us" que quiere decir "vamos a + infinitivo"
lettuce - lechuga
library - biblioteca
license - licencia
like (to) - gustar
line up (to) - formar fila
list - lista
little - pequeño
littler - más pequeño
littlest - el más pequeño
live (to) - vivir
  I live - vivo
  you live - vives; vive
  he, she, it lives - vive
  we live - vivimos
  you (plural) live - vivís
  they live - viven
  living - viviendo
loaf - pan
long - largo
lots - muchos
love (to)- amar
lunch - almuerzo

M

make (to) - hacer
  making - haciendo
man - hombre

many - muchos
margarine - margarina
market - mercado
math - matemáticas
mathematics - matemáticas
me - me; a mí
meat - carne
medicine - medicina
meet (to) - conocer; reunirse
men - hombres
milk - leche
Miss - señorita
mom - mamá
Monday - lunes
money - dinero
more - más
morning - mañana
mother - madre
motor - motorizado
mouth - boca
move - mudarse
movie - cine
Mr. - señor
Mrs. - señora
much - mucho
multiplication - multiplicación
museum - museo
my - mi, mis; mío, míos

N

name - nombre
named - llamado
near - cerca
need (to) - necesitar
new - nuevo
next - próximo
nice - simpático
night - noche; nocturno
nine - nueve
no - no

not - no
now - ahora
number - número

O

o'clock [of the clock] - una contracción de "of the clock" que quiere decir "del reloj"
of - de
office - oficina
O.K. - bien; ¡Bueno!
older - mayor
on - en; encima de
one - uno
onion - cebolla
only - solamente
or - o
orange - naranja; anaranjado
order - orden
other - otro
our - nuestro
out - fuera; afuera
own - propio

P

paper - papel
part - parte
pass (to) - pasar
pay (to)- pagar
penny - centavo
people - personas
persecuted - perseguía
person - persona
personal pronoun - pronombre personal
phone - teléphono
place - lugar

play - jugar
   I play - juego
   you play - juegas; juega
   he, she, it plays - juega
   we play - jugamos
   you (plural) play - jugáis
   they play - juegan
   playing - jugando
please - por favor
plural - plural
popular - popular
potato - papa
practice - práctica
pretty - bonito
pronoun - pronombre
purple - morado
put (to) - poner

Q

R

read (to) - leer
reading - lectura
really - en realidad
recess - recreo
red - rojo
religion - religión
represent - representa
restaurant - restaurante
review - repaso
Right! - ¡Bien!
ring (to) - sonar
road - camino
rock - roca
room - cuarto
rope - cuerda

S

same - mismo
sandwich - sandwiche
Saturday - sábado
say (to) - decir
school - escuela
season - estación; temporada
see (to) - ver
set the table (to) - poner la mesa
seven - siete
she - ella
she's [she is] - una contracción de
   "she is" que quiere decir "ella es"
   o "ella está"
shirt - camisa
shoe - zapato
should - usado con el mismo sentido
   del verbo deber; verbo auxiliar
shopping mall -
showing - demostrando
sick - enfermo
sicker - más enfermo
sickest - el más enfermo
sign - señal
singular - singular
sister - hermana
sit (to) - sentarse
six - seis
skirt - falda
sleep (to) - dormir
   I sleep - duermo
   you sleep - duermes; duerme
   he, she, it sleeps - duerme
   we sleep - dormimos
   you (plural) sleep - dormís
   they sleep - duermen
   sleeping - durmiendo
small - pequeño
smaller - más pequeño
smallest - el más pequeño
so - entonces
soccer - fútbol

soda - refresco
some - alguno; unos
son - hijo
soup - sopa
Spanish - español
star – estrella
start (to) - empezar
stay (to) - quedarse
stay in bed (to) - guardar cama
steak - bistec
stop (to) - detenerse
store - tienda
　　7-ll - unos mercados pequeños en
　　los Estados Unidos
story - historia
student - estudiante
study (to) - estudiar
　　I study - estudio
　　you study - estudias; estudia
　　he, she, it studies - estudia
　　we study - estudiamos
　　you (plural) study - estudiáis
　　they study - estudian
　　studying - estudiando
subject - materia; sujeto
suit - traje
Sunday - domingo
supermarket - supermercado
swim (to) - nadar

T

table - mesa
taco - taco
take (to) - tomar
take off (to) - quitarse
talk (to) - hablar
tax - impuesto
tea - té
teacher - maestro
teeth - dientes

telephone - teléfono
television - televisión
tell (to) - decir
temperature - temperatura
ten - diez
test - examen
thank you - gracias
　　thanks - gracias
that - ese, eso, aquel
that's [that is] - una contracción de
　　"that is" que quiere decir "eso es"
　　o "esa es"
the - el, la, lo, los, las
their - su, sus (de ellos)
them - los, las
then - entonces; luego
there - allá
there's [there is] - una contracción
　　de "there is" que quiere decir
　　"hay"
therefore - por eso
they - ellos
thing - cosa
think (to) - pensar
thirsty - tener sed
this - este, esta, esto
those - aquellos
three - tres
Thursday - jueves
ticket - boleto
time - tiempo
times - por
to - a
toast - pan tostado
today - hoy
tomato - tomate
tomorrow - mañana
too - también
touch (to) - tocar
toy - juguete
traffic - tráfico
travel (to) - viajar

trip - viaje
Tuesday - martes
TV - televisión
two - dos

U

United States - Estados Unidos
until - hasta
up - arriba
use (to) - usar

V

vegetable - legumbre
vehicle - vehículo
very - muy
visit - visita
visit (to) - visitar
vocabulary – vocabulario
vote (to) - votar

W

walk (to) - andar
want (to) - querer
watch (to) - mirar
    I watch - miro
    you watch - miras; mira
    he, she, it watches - mira
    we watch - miramos
    you (plural) watch - miráis
    they watch - miran
    watching - mirando
water - agua
watermelon - sandía
we - nosotros
Wednesday - miércoles
week - semana
well! - ¡bueno!

what - lo que
what? - ¿qué?; ¿cuál?
when - cuando
when? - ¿cuándo?
where - donde
where? - ¿dónde?
which - lo que; lo cual
which? - ¿cuál?
white - blanco;
whiter - más blanco
whitest - el más blanco
who - que; quien
who? - ¿que?; ¿quién?; ¿quiénes?
why? - ¿por qué?
wife - esposa
winter - invierno
with - con
woman - mujer
women - mujeres
word - palabra
work - trabajo
work (to) - trabajar
    I work - trabajo
    you work - trabajas; trabaja
    he, she, it works - trabaja
    we work - trabajamos
    you (plural) work - trabajáis
    they work - trabajan
    working - trabajando
would - verbo auxiliar usado para
    denotar el condicional
wow! - ¡caramba!
write (to) - escribir
written exam - examen escrito

X

Y

year - año

yellow - amarillo
yellower - más amarillo
yellowest - el más amarillo
yes - sí
yet - ya
you - tú, usted, ustedes
you're [you are] - una contracción
    de "you are" que quiere decir "tú
    eres, tú estás; usted es, usted
    está; vosotros estáis, vosotros
    sois; ustedes son, ustedes están"
younger - menor
your - tu, tus; su, sus

Z

Dictionary * Diccionario

Spanish - English * Español – Inglés

A

a - to, on
abajo - below
abarrotes - groceries
abrelatas - can opener
acción - action
acerca de - about
acostarse - to go to bed
adelante - forward; ahead
   en adelante - from now on
adjetivo - adjective
aeroplano - airplane
afuera - out; outside
agua - water
ahora - now
al [a + el] - to the
álbum - album
algún(o) - some
allá - there; over there
almuerzo - lunch
alto - high
amar - to love
amarillo - yellow
americano - American
amigo - friend
anaranjado - orange
andar - to walk
antes - before
   antes de - before
añadir - to add
año - year
apóstrofe - apostrophe
aprender - to learn
apurarse - to hurry up
aquel, aquello - that one

aquellos - those
aquí - here
arte - art
autobús - bus
avión - airplane
ayuda - help
ayudar - to help
azul - blue

B

baño - bath
   traje de baño - bathing suit
barco - boat
bebé - baby
beber - to drink
béisbol - baseball
biblioteca - library
bien - well
¡bien! - good; O.K.
bistec - steak
blanco - white
blusa - blouse
boca - mouth
boleto - ticket
bonito - pretty
brincar - to jump
   brincar la cuerda - to jump rope
buen(o) - good
   buenos días - good morning

C

cada - each; every
café - brown; coffee
caja - box

California - a state in the United States
cama - bed
    guardar cama - to stay in bed
cambiar - to change
cambio - change
camino - road
camisa - shirt
campana - bell
campo - field
capital - capital
¡caramba! - wow!
caricaturas - cartoons
carne - meat
carro - car
casa - house
catarro - cold
cebolla - onion
celebrar - to celebrate
cena - dinner
cenar - to have dinner
cepillar - to brush
cerca - nearby
cerveza - beer
cien - one hundred
cinco - five
cincuenta - fifty
cine - movie
cita - appointment; date
ciudad - city
colonos - colonists
color - color
coma - comma
comer - to eat
comida - meal
comillas - quotation marks
como - as; like
¿cómo? - how?
comparación - comparison
componerse de - to be composed of
compra - purchase

ir de compras - to go shopping
comprar - to buy
compró - he bought; she bought
común - common
con - with
conducir - to drive
conductor - driver
conocer - to meet; to know
consonante - consonant
contracción - contraction
conversación - conversation
cosa - thing
costar - to cost
costoso - expensive
cual - which
    lo cual - that which
¿cuál? - which one?; what?
¿cuánto? - how much?
¿cuántos? - how many?
cuarto - fourth
cuatro - four
cuerda - rope
cuidado - care
    con cuidado - carefully
cupón - coupon

Ch

chaqueta - chaqueta
cheque - check
chequera - checkbook
chimenea - fireplace
chocolate - chocolate

D

dar - to give
de - of; from
de veras - truly
deber - to have to

decidir - to decide
decir - to say; to tell
declarar - to declare
del [de + el] - of the
delicioso - delicious
demostrando - showing
departamento - department
    Departamento de Vehículos Motorizados - Department of Motor Vehicles
depender - to depend
derecha - right side
desayuno - breakfast
desembarcar - to land
después - after; afterwards
día - day
    día de fiesta - holiday
diálogo - dialogue
dientes - teeth
diez - ten
difícil - difficult
dinero - money
Dios - God
directo - direct
distinto - different
DMV - Department of Motor Vehicles
doble - double
doctor - doctor
    Dr. - abbreviation of doctor
dólar - dollar
domingo - Sunday
donde - where
¿dónde? - where?
dormir - to sleep
dos - two
durante - during
durar - to last
duro - hard

E

edificio - building
ejecuta - executes
ejemplo - example
el - the
él - he
ella - she
ello - it
ellos - they
empezar - to start
en - in
enamorado - boyfriend
encargar - in charge
encontrar - to find
enfermo - sick
enfrente - in front
ensalada - salad
enseñar - to show
entonces - then
entre - between
era - he was; she was; it was
eran - they were
es - he is; she is; it is
escribir - to write
escuela - school
ese - that
eso - that
    eso es - that's [that is]
espacio - space
español - Spanish
esposa - wife
esta - this
estación - season
estado - state
estar - to be
este - this
esto - this
estudiante - student
estudiar - to study
etc. - et cetera
exacto - exact
examen - test; exam

examinar - to examine
excelente - excellent

F

facilidad - facility
   tener facilidad para - to be good at
falda - skirt
familia - family
favor - favor
   favor de - please
   por favor - please
favorito - favorite
fecha – date
feliz - happy
fiebre - fever
fiesta - holiday
fila - row
forma - form; shape
formar - to form
   formar fila - to line up
frío - cold
fruta - fruit
fue - he went; she went; it went
   se fue - he, she, or it went away
fútbol - soccer
futuro - future

G

galón - gallon
gasolina - gasoline
gasolinera - gas station
gato - cat
gente - people
gobierno - government
gracias - thanks; thank you
grado - degree; grade
grande - big

gripe - flu
guardar cama - to stay in bed
gustar - to like

H

hablar - to speak; to talk
hacer - to do; to make
hamburguesa - hamburger
harina - flour
hasta - until
hay - there is; there are
   hay que - it is necessary
he aquí- here is
hecho - made
helado - ice cream
hermana - sister
hermano - brother
hija - daughter
hijo - son
historia - history; story
¡hola! - hello!
hombre - man
hora - hour
hotel - hotel
hoy - today
huevo - egg

I

iglesia - church
impuesto - tax
indicar - to indicate
infinitivo - infinitive
inglés; inglesa - English
interesante - interesting
interpreta - interprets
ir - to go
irse - to go away

J

juego - game
jueves - Thursday
jugar - to play
juguete - toy

K

L

la - the
lección - lesson
leche - milk
lechuga - lettuce
lectura - reading
leer - to read
legumbre - vegetable
letra - letter
ley - law
libra - pound
libreta - notebook
libro - book
licencia - license
    licencia de manejar - driver's license
limpiar - to clean
lista - list
luego - then
lugar - place
lunes - Monday

Ll

llamar - to call; to name
    llamar por teléfono - to telephone
llamarse - to be called or named
llegar - to come
llenar - to fill in; to fill out
    llene el espacio - fill in the blank

llevar - to bring
llave - key

M

madre - mother
maestro - teacher
mamá - mom
manejar - to drive
manera - manner; way
mano - hand
manual - manual; handbook
manzana - apple
mañana - morning; tomorrow
margarina - margarine
martes - Tuesday
más - more
matemáticas - mathematics; math
materia - subject
mayor - older
mayúscula - capital letter
me - me
medicina - medicine
médico - doctor
mejor - better
memoria - memory
menor - younger
mercado - market
mesa - table
mi - my
miércoles - Wednesday
mío - my; mine
mirar - to look
mismo - self
    para sí mismo - for himself
mitad - half
morado - purple
morir - to die
motor - motor
muchacho - boy
mucho - much; a lot

mudarse - to move
mujer - woman
multiplicación - multiplication
multiplicar - to multiply
muñeca - doll
    casa de muñecas - dollhouse
museo - museum
muy - very

N

nadar - to swim
naranja - orange
náusea - nausea
    tener náuseas - to be sick to ones
    stomach
necesitar - to need
negro - black
ni - neither
nieve - ice cream; snow
niño - child; boy
no - no
noche - night
nocturno - night
nombrado - named
nombrar - to name
nombre - name; noun
nosotros - we
notar - to note; to observe
nuestro - our
nueve - nine
nuevo - new
número - number

Ñ

O

o - or
observar - to observe

obtener - to get
ocho - eight
oficina - office
oído - ear
ojo - eye
omitir - to omit
oración - sentence
otro - another

P

pagar - to pay
país - country
palabra - word
pan – bread, loaf
papa - potato
papel - paper
para - for; in order to
parte - part
pasar - to pass
    pasar lista - to call roll
pegar - to hit
pelo - hair
pelota - ball
pensar - to think
pequeño - little
permitir - to permit; to let
pero - but
perro - dog
perseguía - persecuted
persona - person
pescado - fish
pie - foot
pizarrón - board; blackboard
plátano - banana
playa - beach
plural - plural
poco - little

poder - power; to be able
    poderes - the branches of
    government
pollo - chicken
poner - to put
ponerse - to put on
popular - popular
por - for; times
¿por qué? - why?
porque - because
portarse - to behave
práctica - practice
practicar - to practice
preparar - to prepare
primer(o) - first
pronombre - pronoun
propio - own
próximo - next
puntuación - punctuation

Q

que - that
¿qué? - what?
quedarse - to stay
querer - to want
¿quién? - who?
quitar - to take away
quitarse - to take off

R

ratón - mouse
raya - line
realidad (en) - really
recaer - to fall upon
recámara - bedroom
recordar - to remember
recreo - recess
refresco - soda
regla - rule

regular - regular
religión - religion
repaso - review
representa - represent
respuesta - answer
restaurante - restaurant
reunirse - to meet
roca - rock
rojo - red
ropa - clothes; clothing

R R

S

sábado - Saturday
saber - to know
salir - to go out
sandía - watermelon
sandwiche - sandwich
sección - section
segundo - second
seis - six
semana - week
sentarse - to sit down
sentirse - to feel
señal - sign
señor - Mr.
señora - Mrs.
señorita - Miss
ser - to be
si - if
sí - yes
    sí mismo - himself
siempre - always
siete - seven
siguiente - following
simpático - nice
simplemente - simply
sin - without
singular - singular

sobre - over; on
solamente - only
sombrero - hat
sonar – to ring
sopa - soup
su - your, his, her, its, their
sucio - dirty
sujeto - subject
supermercado - supermarket

T

taco - taco
también - also
tampoco - either
tarde - afternoon
tarea - job; homework
tarjeta - card
taza - cup
te - you
té - tea
telefonear - to telephone
teléfono - telephone
televisión - television
temperatura - temperature
temporada - season
temprano - early
tener - to have
    tener hambre - hungry
    tener náuseas - to be sick to ones
    stomach
    tener que - to have to
    tener sed - thirsty
tercero - third
terminación - end
terminar - to finish
tienda - store
tocar - to touch
tocino - bacon
todo - all

tomar - to take; to drink
tomate - tomato
tostado - toasted
    pan tostado - toast
trabajar - to work
traer - to bring; to take
tráfico - traffic
traje - suit
trece - thirteen
tres - three
tu - your
tú - you

U

un(o) - a, an
uno - one
usar - to use
usted - you
usualmente - usually
uva - grape

V

vehículo - vehicle
venir - to come
ver - to see
veras - truth
verbo - verb
verdaderamente - really
verde - green
vestido - dress
vez - time
viajar - to travel
viaje - trip
viernes - Friday
visita - visit
visitar - to visit
vivir - to live
vocabulario - vocabulary

vosotros - you (plural)
votar (to) - votar

W

Washington, D.C. - the capital of
the United States

X

Y

y - and
ya - already
yo - I

Z

zapato – shoe
zorro - fox

ÍNDICE

INDEX

Books Available From **FISHER HILL**
For Ages 10-Adult

ENGLISH READING COMPREHENSION FOR THE SPANISH SPEAKER Books 1, 2, 3, 4, 5 & 6

ENGLISH READING AND SPELLING FOR THE SPANISH SPEAKER Books 1, 2, 3, 4, 5 & 6

ENGLISH for the SPANISH SPEAKER Books 1, 2, 3, 4 & Cassettes

SPANISH made FUN and EASY Books 1 & 2

HEALTH Easy to Read

UNITED STATES OF AMERICA Stories, Maps, Activities in Spanish and English Books 1, 2, 3, & 4

English Reading Comprehension for the Spanish Speaker Books 1, 2, 3, 4, 5 & 6 contain twenty lessons to help Spanish-speaking students improve their English reading comprehension skills. Lessons include practice with vocabulary, visualization, fluency, phonology, and comprehension. Each lesson has an answer key. These are excellent books to use after completing *English Reading and Spelling for the Spanish Speaker Books 1, 2, 3, 4, & 5*. Price is $15.95, size is 8 1/2 x11 and each book is approximately 161 pages. Book 1 ISBN 978-1-878253-37-8, Book 2 ISBN 978-1-878253-43-9, Book 3 ISBN 978-1-878253-44-6, Book 4 ISBN 978-1-878253-47-7, Book 5 ISBN 978-1-878253-48-4, Book 6 ISBN 978-1-878253-50-7.

English Reading and Spelling for the Spanish Speaker Books 1, 2, 3, 4, 5 & 6 contain twenty lessons to help Spanish-speaking students learn to read and spell English. The books use a systematic approach in teaching the English speech sounds and other phonological skills. They also present basic sight words that are not phonetic. The word lists are in Spanish and English and all directions are in Spanish with English translations. Each book is $14.95 and approximately 142 pages. Book size is 8 1/2 x 11. Book 1 ISBN 978-1-878253-27-9, Book 2 ISBN 978-1-878253-25-5, Book 3 ISBN 978-1-878253-26-2, Book 4 ISBN 978-1-878253-29-3, Book 5 ISBN 978-1-878253-30-9, Book 6 ISBN 978-1-878253-35-4.

ENGLISH for the SPANISH SPEAKER Books 1, 2, 3, & 4 are English as a Second Language workbooks for ages 10 - adult. Each book is divided into eight lessons and is written in Spanish and English. Each lesson includes: vocabulary, a conversation, a story, four activity pages, an answer key, two dictionaries: English-Spanish and Spanish-English, a puzzle section, and an index. Each book is $13.95 and approximately 110 pages. Book size is 8 1/2 x 11. Book 1 ISBN 978-1-878253-07-1, Book 2 ISBN 978-1-878253-53-8, Book 3 ISBN 978-1-878253-17-0, Book 4 ISBN 978-1-878253-52-1; Book 1 Cassette ISBN 978-1-878253-21-7, Book 2 Cassette ISBN 978-1-878253-32-3, Book 3 Cassette ISBN 978-1-878253-33-0, Book 4 Cassette ISBN 978-1-878253-34-7.

SPANISH made FUN and EASY Books 1 & 2 are workbooks for ages 10 - adult. Each book includes stories, games, conversations, activity pages, vocabulary lists, dictionaries, and an index. The books are for beginning Spanish students; people who want to brush up on high school Spanish; or for Spanish speakers who want to learn how to read and write Spanish. Each book is $14.95 and 134 pages. Book size is 8 1/2 x 11. Book 1 ISBN 978-1-878253-42-2, Book 2 ISBN 978-1-878253-46-0.

HEALTH Easy to Read contains 21 easy to read stories. After each story is a vocabulary page, a grammar page, and a question and answer page. The stories are about changing people's life styles to reduce their risk of poor health and premature death. Book is $13.95 and has 118 pages. Book size is 8 1/2 x 11. ISBN 978-1-878253-41-5.

United STATES of America Stories, Maps, Activities in SPANISH and ENGLISH Books 1, 2, 3, & 4 are easy to read books about the United States of America for ages 10 - adult. Each state is presented by a story, map, and activities. Each book contains information for 12 to 13 states and has an answer key and index. The states are presented in alphabetical order. Book size is 8 1/2 x 11. Each book is $14.95 and approximately 140 pages.
Book 1 ISBN 978-1-878253-23-1 Alabama through Idaho
Book 2 ISBN 978-1-878253-11-8 Illinois through Missouri
Book 3 ISBN 978-1-878253-12-5 Montana through Pennsylvania
Book 4 ISBN 978-1-878253-13-2 Rhode Island through Wyoming

Toll Free Ordering
1-800-214-8110
Monday-Friday 8am-5pm
Central Standard Time

Order On-Line
www.Fisher-Hill.com

Fisher Hill

5267 Warner Ave., #166
Huntington Beach, CA 92649-4079
www.Fisher-Hill.com

Purchase Order Number: _____

Bill To:
Name: _____
Address: _____
City: _____ State _____ ZIP _____
Phone: _____

Ship To: (if different than billing address)
Name: _____
Address: _____
City: _____ State _____ ZIP _____
Phone: _____

QUANTITY	ISBN	BOOK TITLE	PRICE	AMOUNT
	37-8	English Reading Comprehension for the Spanish Speaker Book 1	$15.95	
	43-9	English Reading Comprehension for the Spanish Speaker Book 2	$15.95	
	44-6	English Reading Comprehension for the Spanish Speaker Book 3	$15.95	
	47-7	English Reading Comprehension for the Spanish Speaker Book 4	$15.95	
	48-4	English Reading Comprehension for the Spanish Speaker Book 5	$15.95	
	50-7	English Reading Comprehension for the Spanish Speaker Book 6	$15.95	
	27-9	English Reading and Spelling for the Spanish Speaker Book 1	$14.95	
	25-5	English Reading and Spelling for the Spanish Speaker Book 2	$14.95	
	26-2	English Reading and Spelling for the Spanish Speaker Book 3	$14.95	
	29-3	English Reading and Spelling for the Spanish Speaker Book 4	$14.95	
	30-9	English Reading and Spelling for the Spanish Speaker Book 5	$14.95	
	35-4	English Reading and Spelling for the Spanish Speaker Book 6	$14.95	
	07-1	English For The Spanish Speaker Book 1	$13.95	
	21-7	English For The Spanish Speaker Book 1 Cassette	$10.95	
	20-0	English For The Spanish Speaker Book 1 and Cassette	$21.95	
	53-8	English For The Spanish Speaker Book 2	$13.95	
	32-3	English For The Spanish Speaker Book 2 Cassette	$10.95	
	38-5	English For The Spanish Speaker Book 2 and Cassette	$21.95	
	17-0	English For The Spanish Speaker Book 3	$13.95	
	33-0	English For The Spanish Speaker Book 3 Cassette	$10.95	
	39-2	English For The Spanish Speaker Book 3 and Cassette	$21.95	
	52-1	English For The Spanish Speaker Book 4	$13.95	
	34-7	English For The Spanish Speaker Book 4 Cassette	$10.95	
	40-8	English For The Spanish Speaker Book 4 and Cassette	$21.95	
	41-5	HEALTH Easy to Read	$13.95	
	23-1	USA Stories, Maps, Activities in Spanish & English Book 1	$14.95	
	11-8	USA Stories, Maps, Activities in Spanish & English Book 2	$14.95	
	12-5	USA Stories, Maps, Activities in Spanish & English Book 3	$14.95	
	13-2	USA Stories, Maps, Activities in Spanish & English Book 4	$14.95	
	42-2	SPANISH made FUN & EASY Book 1	$14.95	
	46-0	SPANISH made FUN & EASY Book 2	$14.95	
	MW920-7	Diccionario Español-Inglés	$6.50	
	MW852-1	Diccionario de Sinónimos y Antónimos en Inglés	$6.50	
	MW890-3	Juego de Diccionarios	$19.50	
	MW605-3	Dictionary of Basic English	$9.95	
	MW550-6	Advanced Learner's English Dictionary	$29.95	

Credit Card Information
Card Number: _____
Expiration Date: _____
Name: _____
Address: _____
City: _____ State _____ ZIP _____
Phone: _____

TOTAL _____

Add 7.75% for shipments to California addresses. SALES TAX _____

Add 10% of TOTAL for shipping. (Minimum $5.00) SHIPPING _____

PAYMENT _____

BALANCE DUE _____